WALK FREE

WALK FREE

An Uncommon Cure for the Common Heart

Jeff + Klicia,
May God continue
to bless your family
richly.
JoAnne
PV 4:23

JoAnne E. Billison

WinePressPublishing
Great Books, Defined.

WinePress Publishing (PO Box 428, Enumclaw, WA 98022) functions only as book publisher. As such, the ultimate design, content, editorial accuracy, and views expressed or implied in this work are those of the author.

Unless otherwise noted, all Scriptures are taken from the *Holy Bible, New International Version*®, *NIV*®. Copyright © 1973, 1978, 1984 by Biblica, Inc.™ Used by permission of Zondervan. All rights reserved worldwide. www.zondervan.com

Scripture references marked NLT are taken from the *Holy Bible, New Living Translation*, copyright © 1996, 2004, 2007 by Tyndale House Foundation. Used by permission of Tyndale House Publishers, Inc., Carol Stream, Illinois 60188. All rights reserved.

ISBN 13: 978-1-4141-1803-1
ISBN 10: 1-4141-1803-1
Library of Congress Catalog Card Number: 2010905994

CONTENTS

ACKNOWLEDGMENTS

WITH GREAT APPRECIATION, I thank my professors at Multnomah Seminary without whom I could never have written this book: A. Baylis II, C. Blom, D. Brake, V. Clemen, G. Curtis, B. Davis, B. Feil, R. Frost, B. Gasser, T. Hauff, P. Johnson, S. Kim, R. Koivisto, P. Metzger, A. Quist, R. Redman, P. Reeve, J. Robertson, J. Terveen, R. Trautmann, C. Wecks, and J. Wecks. I learned so much from these godly and dedicated men and women. They impacted my life in a powerful way. Many of the principles and concepts they taught are woven into the pages of this book.

I thank my husband, Sam, for allowing me to follow my dream. I would not be able to minister or write without his support and love.

I thank my boys, Tommy and Kevin, who have blessed me in so many ways. Throughout this project, they have showered me with encouragement, love, and tremendous patience. I couldn't have finished this book without their support. Thanks a bunch, guys!

I thank Lorelei Magee, my dear friend who read each chapter… several times! Without her help, I would not have been able to clarify my ideas, concepts, and principles so they would be easier to understand. Lorelei, thanks for contributing your time and insight. Both were appreciated.

To my sister, Janet, and my friend, Leslie, thank you for the encouragement and support you gave me throughout this project. You both kept me moving forward every time I felt overwhelmed and ready to quit.

And I thank Kendra Shaw, who saw in me a soul worth saving. My journey started with her when she took a risk and shared her faith with me. Thank you for introducing me to Jesus!

Ultimately, I thank God. His transformational love fills my heart abundantly more than I could have ever imagined. I am honored to be called his daughter.

To God be the glory forever and ever.

INTRODUCTION

A Majestic Vision

When the world collapses around you, falling into rubble—
There is a Master Architect, in charge of all this trouble.
He has in mind a cathedral, enlargement of your soul;
Making more space for Majesty–with holiness the goal.
In order to do some expansion, he needs to tear apart;
No matter the devastation—Your best interests are in his heart.
So let God build a cathedral that nothing on earth can destroy;
His ways are mysterious, yet perfect—
In the end you will have great joy.
Watch and see with astonishment—the wisdom of his plan;
You will arise a new creation—held in the palm of his hand.

—Janie Seltzer

L ET ME INTRODUCE myself. I am a Christian, but I didn't grow up in a Christian home. I entered the Kingdom of God fully grown, married, and a mother of two. Finding faith after ten years of marriage made my transition into the kingdom a very difficult one. Right away, I faced challenges in my home that

I never dreamed I would face. In addition to those challenges, I discovered personal brokenness issues and sinful attitudes—both of which escalated the level of my anguish. On top of all that, I was an overwhelmed mother of two "high needs" toddler boys. Needless to say, I felt as if my life was a mess. However, I was *hungry* for God and determined not to let anything interfere with my newfound faith. Perhaps my hunger for God made me a likely candidate for leadership. I don't really know, but somewhere in the midst of all my difficulties, God called me into ministry. His call eventually led me to Multnomah Seminary.

The six years I attended seminary turned out to be a bittersweet time in my life. Now don't get me wrong, I loved being in seminary. Every class I took stirred my heart in a profound way. I can honestly say learning about God was definitely the sweetest part of my seminary years. But also during that time, I encountered a lot of adversity, adding some bitter to my sweet experiences.

On occasion, some of the difficulties in my life overwhelmed me. Juggling a difficult marriage, personal brokenness issues, children, and school work would stretch me beyond what I felt I could handle. Juggling my problems left me exhausted, scared, and confused. There were times when I felt as if I were drowning in the messiness of my life. One time in particular, I felt so overwhelmed, I believed that all my problems would be resolved if I just quit Multnomah Seminary. During that time I realized I had to get away, gather my thoughts, and find some rest. So I decided to spend a weekend with my sister. The long drive to her house became a life-changing moment for me—a moment I will never forget.

The day started out like any other day—a little damp from the rain. I'd been living in the Pacific Northwest long enough to know that rain is just something that comes with the beautiful majestic countryside. Not giving it another thought, I gathered my boys, fastened them in their car seats, and hit the road. The drive to my sister's house is not a difficult one, and I've taken it many times before. However, on this particular day, things changed rather quickly. Once I hit the highway, the weather turned from a mild drizzle to a torrential rain that soon became a thick fog. Traffic slowed to a crawl. I could barely see the brake lights on the car in front me. The fog was so thick I lost sight of anything familiar along the road. Eventually, I lost track of where I was on the highway. An hour had passed when I began to hear murmurs from the back seat. My boys were hungry. I was totally unprepared. I hadn't anticipated driving slowly in the fog so I hadn't brought a lot of snacks. I had planned to stop on the way to my sisters and buy us lunch, but there I was, stuck in traffic in the middle of nowhere. My attempts to persuade my boys to hang on a little while longer failed, and their murmurs soon became wails. It wasn't long before I felt stressed. I was driving in open country and had no idea how much farther it was to our lunch destination, so I moved into the right lane and began looking for restaurants. We all saw the diner up ahead. Frustrated and tired from the stop-and-go traffic, I relented to my children's cries of hunger and pulled off the highway. I knew deep down inside this was a mistake, but I discounted my feelings and headed for the diner anyway. The place looked run down, but we were determined to make the best of it. I took a deep breath and opened the front door. A thick cloud of cigarette smoke hit us in the face. My oldest cried, "My eyes are burning," and my youngest replied, "I don't care, I'm hungry." My nerves were shot and I just wanted to sit down and decompress.

I looked back at the road. It was still immersed in fog and rain. There was no other restaurant in sight, so I decided to stay. I asked for the non-smoking section and walked with my boys to the back of the restaurant. We ate our lunch in a dark, dingy, smoke-filled diner.

After finishing our meal, we got back in the car, accepted the foggy conditions, and hit the road again. Just a few more miles up the highway the fog miraculously lifted and I saw a road sign that read, "Centralia—4 miles." Centralia had been our intended lunch destination. I was crushed. If I had just stayed on the road a little longer, if I had just endured the pressure I felt to find a restaurant, if I had just pushed through my own flailing emotions a bit more, my boys and I would have had a much better lunch and a healthier atmosphere to eat it in. If, if, if...*if only I had stayed on the road.*

This lesson became a life-changing moment for me because God used it to speak truth into my life. After the shock of realizing how close I had been to Centralia, he touched my heart and gently reminded me that when we remove ourselves from our present circumstances, and exert our own strength to find a pain-free solution, we end up adding misery to our situation. I felt God tugging on my heart that day, challenging me to *stay the course* of my life regardless of the uncertainty I was facing. He assured me that if I would persevere through the confusing, uncomfortable, and painful moments, *I would* find clarity, peace, and blessing.

I made a commitment to God that day. I would face any obstacles that blocked my path. This was no minor commitment on my part. My plate was full of issues that had to be dealt with, but none of that mattered anymore because God reached down and touched my heart in a miraculous way. He used my experience driving in the fog to get my attention and keep me on track. He encouraged me to stay in school, endure my difficulties, and trust him with the uncertainty of my future.

My adventure driving in the fog reminds me of how quickly we become tired and weary when faced with challenging circumstances. So often we grow exhausted from the battle at hand, and in a moment of desperation move off the road we are traveling in order to find immediate comfort. We make life-changing decisions based on what we feel we need at the moment. For example, a young married couple may believe that divorce is the only way out of their marital problems. A broken trust between business partners may cause one to isolate and work alone indefinitely. An overbearing boss may lead one to quit a fulfilling job. Countless others seek various forms of comfort in things like drugs, alcohol, pornography, eating, overworking, compulsive shopping, and so on. Because we don't like our circumstances, we seek comfort and make life-changing decisions in order to *escape* the reality of our situations. Unfortunately, when in escape mode, we give up on our dreams, believing them unattainable. We also convince ourselves that our means of escape will bring rest, but in actuality they increase our pain because deep down we continue feeling unfulfilled. Eventually, we end up believing that our broken, unfulfilling life is as good as our life can ever be. This belief compels us to continue escaping our pain.

Avoiding difficulties in life causes us to circumvent our opportunity to learn and grow from experience. Truly, our failure to travel far enough or long enough *through* a difficult event leaves us spiritually and emotionally underdeveloped. You see, our resolve is strengthened every time we experience an uncomfortable event and stay with it from beginning to end. Without this strength, we end up stuck in a pattern of escaping over and over again because our inexperience leaves us susceptible to false assumptions and "what if" scenarios. In other words, the moment turbulent times hit, we assume the worst and imagine "what if" this happens or "what if" that happens. With this mindset, we easily discourage ourselves from walking through a difficult circumstance, and end up frantically looking for a way around the obstacle in our path. This is how difficult circumstances trap us and prevent us from growing in our faith.

The greatest tragedy of all is the fact that when we escape our pain, we allow our difficulties to blind us to the hope we have been given in Christ. Without hope, we stop growing, stop taking risks, stop persevering, and begin to just exist. Simply speaking, our avoidance of all hardships in life makes us settle for less than the abundant life Christ promised to give to those who believe (John 10:10).

An abundant life in Christ is not a perfect life devoid of suffering. It is a life filled with meaning and hope. An abundant life is one that includes both good and bad days. When our lives take a downward turn, we aren't to avoid the experience, but meet it with truth. Pain and hardship are part of life, and we must allow ourselves to experience them because they are powerful tools used by God to develop our faith, build up our character, and so much more.

The truth is that we are a wealthy nation full of people who have lost the ability to endure hardships. The American church has enabled this position by reinforcing the message that success equals health, wealth, and prosperity. In our efforts to appear successful, we stuff the pain, hide our sin, escape reality, and live out the illusion of a perfect life. But our illusions are unfulfilling and they keep us running toward our means of escape.

Deep spiritual and emotional growth happens in our lives when we face difficulties utterly dependent upon God. Learning to live dependent upon God is vital to our generation. In addition to maneuvering personal and relational struggles, we also have to face some of the most difficult economic times in our country since the Great Depression. People have been laid off from work, a wide variety of illnesses run rampant, and natural disasters are on the rise in all countries, giving us far more to worry about than in any other generation.

Now, more than ever, we must learn how to cling to God with all our might. We need to learn how to endure our difficulties, and develop our faith. Above all else, we must *not* abandon the hope we have been given in Christ.

Getting back to my story, I can honestly say that walking through my difficulties was no easy task. I had both good and bad days. But in the end, it was all worth it. I can unequivocally say that I am the woman I am today because of what I have endured.

And I am so grateful to God for guiding me through the purifying process, because I have never felt so free before.

My life is not an easy one because the growth process is never ending, but I can say that it is an abundant one. I enjoy being with God! He has filled me with strength, courage, joy, and the sweetest intimate relationship with him I have ever known. I live in the truth and reality of my circumstances, and because of this I am able to work with God in the process of transforming my heart.

Healing and walking free are a choice. We must decide if we truly want to be healed and walk in freedom. When our brokenness is discovered, we have a decision to make: Do we deal with the issue or escape the pain? Healing the brokenness of our souls takes time, patience, and persistence. In other words, real effort is involved. We either choose to put forth the effort or choose to escape the pain.

This book provides biblical tools that help you choose to deal with the truth rather than escape it. I have fashioned this book after an eight-week class I developed to teach men and women the life principles God taught me. I use these principles to help men and women become more self-aware and God-dependent. In doing so, I reveal issues of the heart that interfere with our faith.

To Walk Free is a way of life that frees us to become all we can be in Christ. To undertake this lifestyle, we must first understand how our past issues and attitudes have enslaved our hearts. Understanding our enslavement is very important because when left unseen, the enslaving issues control us and prevent us from seeing the truth. With a little heart exploration and help from the Holy Spirit, our blinders can come off and we can achieve transformation.

In order to help personalize the reading, I have included reflective questions, starter prayers, and personal stories from individuals I have either taught or counseled in the past. I have changed the names of the individuals mentioned in order to protect those who graciously gave me permission to share their struggles. I hope their stories will be an encouragement to you.

Make no mistake, dealing with issues of the heart takes real effort on our part, but the effort will be rewarded in the end. The work involved will not be in vain. Spiritual growth, personal strength, and intimacy with God will be your prize!

Please know that not every issue in your life will be resolved immediately as you read through this book. This book is merely a guide to help you tap into God's strength and power. He repairs our brokenness at a time when he knows we can handle the truth.

However, those who participated wholeheartedly have been unbelievably transformed. I have seen men and women move from anxiety, hopelessness, and depression into tumultuous joy as they learned how to *willingly* open their hearts to God. Living in the light of the truth, utterly dependent upon God, is what it means to *walk by faith*.

Now I want to challenge you and encourage you *to stay the course* and read the entire book. Each chapter builds upon the previous one. If the truth within the pages of this book causes fear or pain that entices you to retreat, DON'T QUIT! Keep moving forward. I realize that dealing with the heart can be a very emotional experience. Trust God through this process. Perhaps he is already directing you to the answers you seek by having you read this book. Be encouraged, because no matter what is going on in your life, he who started a good work in you will continue it indefinitely (Phil. 1:6).

To God be the glory as you begin this journey of learning how to *walk free*.

Chapter 1

THE HEART: OUR CENTER OF LIFE

The way to heaven is ascending;
we must be content to travel uphill,
though it be hard and tiresome,
and contrary to the natural bias of our flesh.
—Jonathan Edwards

STACY WAS A faithful follower of Christ. She was married to a loving Christian man, had two wonderful children, and lived in a beautiful home. She mastered the look of success on the outside, but on the inside, was tormented by fears and anxiety. She felt as if a pit were growing in the center of her stomach and slowly engulfing her life. The more anxious she became, the harder she worked at covering up her emotions until she could no longer bear it. Deep down in her heart, Stacy felt alone—distant from God and depressed. Little difficulties in life soon became overwhelming obstacles for her to maneuver. As Stacy and I unpacked some of the issues hidden deep within her heart, she was able to see how they had shaped her life. Unbeknownst to her, those issues had hardened her heart toward God, preventing his healing touch. By bringing her issues to the surface, Stacy was able to heal.

Healing came as she learned how to open herself up to God. This involved developing some new habits like daily prayer, reading scripture, embracing scriptural truths, and fostering an intimate relationship with God. Stacy's life was transformed because she experienced God's love.

As Stacy walked through this process, she gained confidence, strength, and self-assurance. And most importantly, the pit she felt growing in the center of her stomach disappeared completely. She is like a new woman, and she no longer fears the challenges in her life.

OUR HEARTS

With great wisdom, Solomon writes, "Above all else we must protect our hearts for they affect everything we do" (Prov. 4:23 NLT). Very simply speaking, the heart is part of our inner being or *soul*. The great theologian Jonathan Edwards (1703-1758) describes our soul as having two parts: the heart and the mind. The heart is our spiritual center and the mind is our thinking center. The heart consists of our personality, desires, passions, loves, hates, emotions, and will. Basically, the essence of what makes us who we are comes directly from our hearts. But the heart does not operate alone; we must also include the mind. The mind handles perception, discernment, knowledge, thinking, and judgment. The heart and the mind are intimately connected, forming our spiritual self or soul. Our spiritual self and physical self (body) are fused together, making up what is often defined as the "whole person." Though we exist as beings formed by our minds, hearts, and bodies, Solomon points out that our hearts affect everything we do. Ultimately, our hearts have a greater influence over our thoughts and actions.

More than seven hundred Bible verses mention the heart. This massive amount of scripture involving the heart suggests the significant role it plays in our everyday life. Here are a few examples of what the Bible teaches us about our hearts:

- Deuteronomy 4:29: "You will find God if you look for him with all your heart and with all your soul," meaning when we seek God with a deep earnest desire, he will reveal himself to us.
- Deuteronomy 6:5: "Love the Lord your God with all your heart and with all your soul and with all your strength," meaning our *whole body*, the spiritual and physical person, is to love God with a deep, intimate love.
- Deuteronomy 8:2: "Remember how the Lord your God led you all the way in the desert these forty years, to humble you and to test you in order to know what was in your heart, whether or not you would keep his commandments," meaning God humbles and tests us in order to reveal whether or not we truly love him. Our obedience to his ways, especially in the face of adversity, demonstrates our love for him.
- Matthew 15:16-19: Jesus teaches about the heart by saying, "Don't you see that whatever enters the mouth goes into the stomach and then out of the body? But the things that come out of the mouth come from the heart, and these make a man unclean. For out of the heart come evil thoughts, murder, adultery, sexual immorality, theft, false testimony, slander," meaning our hearts are responsible for evil thoughts, destructive attitudes, actions of wickedness, and immoral behaviors.

In the story above, the broken condition of Stacy's heart was slowly destroying her life. As she came to understand the issues in her heart, she began to heal. Understanding the condition of our hearts is crucial if we are to achieve freedom in Christ.

COMMUNICATION TO THE HEART

The heart is the most important part of our being. It influences everything we do. If we want to hear God's voice and learn his ways, then we need to consider the condition of our hearts.

When God communicates with us, he communicates to our hearts because the heart is the center of our spiritual being. We love God simply because he has captivated our hearts first with his love (1 John 4:19). The apostle Paul wrote, "That hope does not disappoint us because God has poured out his love into our hearts by the Holy Spirit" (Rom. 5:5). This outpouring of love in our hearts is what ultimately draws us closer to God.

When our hearts are captivated by God's love, we respond in kind with love, obedience, sharing our testimonies, and growing in faith. However, when God's outpouring of love is hindered in our hearts, our ability to experience his love diminishes, resulting in a tendency to shrink back, grumble, and feel spiritually dry. Harmful attitudes and unresolved issues in life are our greatest hindrance to receiving God's love. The reason for this is that these issues harden our hearts.

In the *Dictionary of Jesus and the Gospels*, a soft heart is described as "being receptive to the divine will; whereas a hard heart is not."[1] Since God is communicating to our hearts, our ability to be receptive to the desires of *his heart* is directly related to the condition of our hearts. This means that the harder our hearts are, the less likely we can understand the ways of God or experience his love.

A simple analogy of a hard heart is like comparing a sponge with a stone. When water is poured over a sponge, the sponge being very soft and pliable is able to absorb the water. When that same water is poured over a stone, only miniscule particles of water are absorbed, and the majority runs off the stone.

If our hearts are soft, we absorb God's outpouring of love like a sponge. We also gain comfort and understanding. However, if our hearts are hard, most of God's outpouring of love rolls off us as if our hearts were a stone, leaving us spiritually dry and needy. This emptiness compels us to find our own way to manage and control our lives.

When it comes to understanding a hard heart, it is interesting to note that Jesus accused both the Pharisees and his disciples of being hard hearted (Mark 3:5; 6:52; 8:17-21). Jesus often called the Pharisees hypocrites, fools, and blind guides, pointing to their unbelief as rendering them dull to hearing God's Word. The disciples, on the other hand, did not necessarily suffer from unbelief, but from moments of little faith combined with confusion. In our Christian walk, we struggle with a little bit of everything—little faith, confusion, and unbelief.

This is why we must dig deep into the matters of our hearts. We need to discover what we are harboring so we can challenge ourselves to stand up against any negative attitudes and seek healing for painful issues.

THE INFLUENCE OF A BROKEN HEART

As the center or core of our spiritual being, the heart is a very powerful influence upon our bodies. What affects the heart will inevitably affect the course or direction of our life. Jesus illustrated this point when he said that whatever fills the heart is what comes out of the mouth. A good man expresses and behaves in a good manner, and an evil man expresses and behaves in an evil manner (Matt. 12:34-35). In other words, the condition of the heart determines how well we react to life's circumstances. If our hearts are healthy, we are capable of responding with goodness and love. However, if our hearts are full of sinful attitudes and hidden pain, we are equally capable of responding with acts of evil, anger, and hatred. Jesus points this out again in his discussion with the Pharisees over clean and unclean foods (Mark 7:17-23). He clearly states that nothing taken into the body will make one unclean, for these things go into the stomach and are eliminated. But man is corrupted by the attitudes that come out of his heart. For out of the heart come evil thoughts, thefts, coveting, wickedness, deceit, sensuality, envy, slander, pride, foolishness—and the list continues. Think about the time someone cut you off in traffic, you didn't get to do things your way at work, or your friend showed you his brand new Apple iPhone. What thoughts popped into your head? Guess where those thoughts came from…your heart. The more clearly we understand the condition of our hearts, the better equipped we are to discern attitudes and life-shaping influences that creep out.

The apostle Paul gives us another picture of the heart. As he wraps up his first letter to the Thessalonians, he commands the believers to live faithfully (1 Thess. 5:14-22). He uses verbs written with a present active imperative form, indicating that believers are commanded to actively pursue these directives as a habit of daily life.

One of these directives states, "Do not quench the Spirit" (1 Thess. 5:19). In this verse, the word "quench" means to stifle or suppress. Therefore, the command is telling us *not* to suppress the Holy Spirit's influence in our lives. In another passage Paul also commands that we not *grieve* (present active imperative form) the Holy Spirit (Eph. 4:30). These two passages teach us a great deal about the human power and strength we have within our hearts. These passages tell us we are capable of overriding God's divine presence in us. Clearly, *we have the ability to suppress the Holy Spirit's influence in our lives.*

Here's how this works in real life. When we find ourselves in the midst of a difficult situation and our hearts are hard, we tend to override the Holy Spirit's influence guiding us to endure a hardship in favor of avoiding the pain and restoring peace by whatever means necessary. As we flee discomfort, we control our circumstances and fix our situations by exerting our own desires and strength. For many of us, fixing our situation involves controlling the people in our lives as well. We become controlling in order to feel in control. The more controlling we become, the harder our hearts become, interfering with our ability to grow dependent upon God. Our lack of God-dependency results in our failure to trust him completely with our lives, which ultimately leads us to foster a superficial faith. When our faith is superficial, we fail to understand the ways of God or the purpose in our suffering.

Because we can easily suppress the Holy Spirit's influence in our hearts, we must slow down and take the time needed to look into the condition of our hearts. Bottom line, if we suppress the Holy Spirit, the reality of our Christian walk is a walk by the *flesh* (by our own strength) and not by the Spirit.

To fully understand this point, we must consider two other key elements connected with the heart: The desires of our flesh and our emotions.

THE DESIRES OF OUR FLESH

When Scripture mentions our flesh, it generally means our physical body. But the apostle Paul gave the word a deeper meaning. He often used the word to describe the corruptible nature of our earthly lives. Due to the fall of mankind, humanity became vulnerable to immoral or unethical desires of the body. Because our body is fused with our soul, our "whole being" is involved in everything we do. This is why we often find ourselves stuck wrestling against the sinful desires of our flesh. This wrestling of our flesh can be very intense. The alcoholic struggling to stop drinking, the workaholic struggling to cut back his hours, the depressed struggling to maneuver their way through life, and the perfectionist attempting to be less than perfect are all examples of intense battles taking place within us. When we fail to take an internal look at the status of our hearts, by default, we fall prey to the desires of our flesh.

I believe we genuinely desire to worship God with all our hearts. Nevertheless, living as a broken person in a broken world naturally sets us up to be enslaved to many aspects of our flesh. Struggles with addictions like overeating, pornography, alcohol, and compulsive shopping are a few of the areas where we become grievously aware of our bondage. These areas often become obvious places of concentrated work. However, something far more damaging to our Christian walk comes from areas that exist in our unconsciousness. These are the areas hidden deep within our hearts that need to be brought to our attention by the Holy Spirit.

Our life in Christ is a process of perfecting our Christian walk. Though we may be at different places along the path that makes up this process, we are all in process. Part of this process involves revealing areas of hardness in our hearts so those issues can be dealt with and we can "die" to the sinful desires they produce.

Gratifying the flesh takes us away from God and leaves us spiritually dry. In Romans 8, the apostle Paul passionately tells us to live by the Spirit and not by the flesh. To help us understand his point, Paul describes the different desires taking shape in the hearts of those who walk by the flesh, versus those who walk by the Spirit. The chart on the top of page 9 is drawn out of this passage and may help illustrate what Paul is describing.

Allowing our flesh to rule our lives ultimately causes us to oppose God and his ways. If we continue placating our flesh, we stay spiritually weak and vulnerable to our own unhealthy sinful desires. The more we understand the issues afflicting our hearts, the more we can manage and address the corruptible nature of our flesh.

A life according to the flesh	A life according to the Spirit
Weak	*Strong*
• Has a mind that is focused on things that make the body or self happy. • Closed to the influence of the Holy Spirit—stands in opposition to God and reflects hatred or hostility toward godly ways. • Unable to live in a manner pleasing to God because personal desires get in the way. • Leads to death.	• Has a mind that is focused on things that make God happy. • Open to the influence of the Spirit of God dwelling within—stands in line with God and godly ways. • Has the ability to live in a manner pleasing to God because the Holy Spirit has given new life to the body through righteousness. • Leads to life and peace.

OUR EMOTIONS

Our emotions are intense feelings seated deep within our hearts. They are part of the image God gave mankind. Emotions help define us as human beings and distinguish us from one another. They help us feel things like joy, laughter, love, peace, and pleasure. They also help us sense dangerous situations and people. Unfortunately, emotions like fear, hatred, sorrow, and pain can leave an indelible imprint upon our hearts, seriously impeding our Christian walk.

The emotions surrounding unresolved issues, fears, past hurts, or attitudes submerged deep within our hearts leave wounds or calluses behind. Any time new circumstances trigger these deeply submerged wounds, we unconsciously react to the pain again. Since the issues were never resolved, our flesh persuades us to protect ourselves from feeling hurt. This is why we feel the desire to conceal, stuff, and keep a lid on the emotions that cause our discomfort. We repeat the stuffing process every time the same sets of wounds are triggered. As we continue stuffing the pain in our hearts, they harden until we stop feeling altogether.

It works like this: The emotions surrounding our broken hearts send messages to our brains, creating new pathways designed to protect us from feeling pain. Ultimately, these pathways affect the way we react to our circumstances and view life. Just as a coffee filter prevents the coffee grounds from getting into the coffee, our behavioral pathways are patterns of behavior that prevent pain from touching our lives. Unfortunately, these pathways harden our hearts and move us away from God. Furthermore, they become controlling factors influencing our decision-making processes, resulting in miscommunications and frequent misunderstandings. The following example demonstrates how our emotions and hearts influence our interactions with people.

At a business meeting, Stan let everyone know how important it was that they work together to achieve their goal. Everyone's job was essential to the outcome of the product. If someone failed to do his or her job in an appropriate amount of time, it could delay the others on the team and ultimately delay the release date for the product. Everyone was given a special piece of the production cycle, and Stan asked them to check in with him periodically so he could review the work and assess how close they were to achieving their production goal. Stan urged the team to work together in order to support and help one another accomplish their objective.

Stan honestly intended to encourage his team to support one another, and the deadline he was given. Dick grumbled as he walked away from the meeting feeling pressured to work harder with longer hours and no additional pay. Amy preferred to work alone. She walked away from the meeting feeling anxious that Stan wanted to control her work and creativity. Tim loved working under pressure and was excited to be a part of the team. He eagerly sought Stan out to discuss some of his ideas.

Each of these people interpreted the meeting differently because they each had different past issues triggered. As their minds processed the information they received, their emotions touched unresolved issues deep within their hearts, stirring their desires for protection from the pain. The behavioral pathways in their heads caused each of them to react differently to Stan's intent, ultimately giving them different perspectives of the meeting.

Bottom line, our unresolved past issues become oozing wounds that stir in our hearts as current circumstances trigger our emotions. The more our emotions are stirred, the more we reinforce the use of our behavioral patterns or pathways. Our emotions indirectly cause us to distort the truth and increase the pain in our lives.

Here is another example: Tami was part of the worship team at her church. She had a beautiful voice and a desire to sing for the Lord. However, the past hurts in her life created a behavioral pathway that caused her to misinterpret the worship leader's decisions. Though he appreciated her singing voice and contribution to the worship team, he would not perform the songs she suggested. He tried to explain why her songs would not work at their church, but she failed to understand. She began to struggle emotionally with being a member of the team and felt like quitting. As we talked about the issues in her heart, we discovered she had a very controlling father during childhood. His excessive control over her as a child created a wound in her heart that developed a need for protection from being controlled. The rejection of her songs by the worship leader triggered this wound, making her feel vulnerable. Internally, she felt herself being controlled, and that created a great deal of tension within her.

Once Tami realized that her emotions were triggered by her fear of being controlled, she was able to put everything into perspective.

Healing came as she brought her fears to the surface and opened her heart to receive God's healing touch. As she began to trust God with her situation and her feelings, she realized that the worship leader's rejection of her songs had nothing to do with her. She could see that his intent was not to control her, but to manage the worship sessions at her church. Tami grew in confidence as she grew dependent upon the Lord. Her dependence on God eventually led her to leave the worship team she was on, not because of her emotions, but because she no longer believed God wanted her on that team. Because she endured this difficult situation and gave up her heart's desire to sing, she grew even more dependent upon God for her wellbeing. As she grew closer to God, He eventually chose her to lead worship in a new church. Now she is not only singing the songs she wants, but God also helps her write new ones.

Our emotions are powerful tools that are used to guide us through life. When they are triggered in the midst of circumstances, they tell us something is going on deep within our hearts. If we take the time to listen, ask God to reveal truth, and prepare ourselves to endure the pain of working through our issues, emotions can become instruments of healing and strength. God meets us in the seat of our emotions deep within our hearts. We need only be willing to *feel* (our emotions) in order to commune with him there.

SUMMING IT ALL UP

Our hearts are the center of our spiritual being. The more we understand what is going on in our hearts, the better equipped we are at keeping them healthy, soft, and absorbent of God's outpouring of love.

When we have unresolved hurt, pain, or attitudes in our lives, calluses are developed deep within our hearts, hardening the heart and hindering our ability to understand the ways of God. When our hearts are hard, they resemble stones and repel most of God's love, leaving us spiritually dry and in search of something more. Our attempts to handle the difficult circumstances of life apart from God leave us desperate to find pain-free solutions in order to fix or control our conditions. To restore peace, the hardened heart will seek solutions that either consciously or unconsciously come from the desires of our flesh.

We feel our emotions every time our areas of unresolved issues are touched by current situations. Because our flesh desires to be pain free, emotions connected to unresolved issues in our lives cause us to stuff the pain, conceal the truth, or respond to our circumstances with some behavior in order to help us avoid the hurt. Behavioral pathways developed from our broken hearts wire our brains to set patterns of behavior that are designed to protect us from discomfort. Unfortunately, our patterns of behavior change our perceptions of life by affecting our ability to accurately interpret situations causing miscommunications. The more we appease the desires of our flesh, the more we suppress the Holy Spirit's influence in our life.

We need to understand what is happening inside our hearts so we can identify the desires of our flesh. Pulling away from our flesh is a costly process, as noted by Paul's instructions to "die" to the desires of our flesh. This concept indicates pain and loss. Some of us have lived with hardened hearts for such a long time that a lot of callused tissue has developed. Softening hardness takes time. Patience is needed.

Dying to our flesh feels uncomfortable because we step away from the familiarity and false security of our routines. This can be a stressful process, but I assure you, you will never be alone. God will be with you every step of the way. The first few steps are always the hardest because they break open the lid to our pain we so cleverly try to keep in place. However, if you are willing to walk through the process wholeheartedly, it will be transformational.

Keep in mind the burdens we carry keep us from walking by the Spirit. Our issues can make us feel like we are moving through life carrying a heavy load on our shoulders. As we cling to the weight of our burdens, we unintentionally reject help from the Holy Spirit. When we learn how to release our burdens into the hands of the Holy Spirit, the weight we've carried begins to fade. We are not trying to find some sort of balance between our flesh and the Spirit such as in a ying and yang configuration. The flesh and Spirit do not harmonize. No, we are instructed to die to our flesh (live less of me), and walk with the Spirit (live more by the Spirit within me). Learning to lighten our load teaches us how to die to our flesh and walk by the Spirit. The illustration on page 15 gives us a picture of some of the heavy loads we carry.

Once the issues in our hearts are revealed, the desires of our flesh no longer have the same power to enslave us. Once we understand our hearts, we can learn to identify the circumstances that trigger those wounds, enabling us to make better behavioral choices during times of trouble. In essence, we learn to quench the flesh and walk by the Spirit. Making better choices not only alleviates painful consequences, but also develops God-dependency.

One last point: When our hearts remain full of unresolved issues or attitudes, the choices we make in life come from dependence on self or from our self-sufficiency rather than from dependence on God or God-dependency. As we grow spiritually, we want to decrease the amount of our self-sufficiency and increase the amount of our God-dependency. As we increase our God-dependency, emotions triggered by past experiences or attitudes (like fear) will no longer haunt us. This is not to say that we no longer feel these emotions—we are emotional beings—but the sting within these emotions will be removed. And when the sting is gone, we are set free to become all that God has designed us to be.

Our Emotions trigger
unresolved issues and attitudes.
The desire to be pain-free
causes our flesh to develop
behavioural pathways that
influence how we react and
interpret life's circumstances.

Satisfying the desires of our
flesh suppresses the influence
of the Holy Spirit within us
(1 Thess. 5:19).

As we die to the needs of our flesh, we begin to live by the Spirit.

REFLECTIVE THOUGHT

1. Spend some time in reflective prayer with God. Ask him to prepare you to hear the truth regarding the condition of your heart.

2. Begin a journal, tracking your emotions and the way you respond to critical situations. This will help you identify how you react to difficulties in life. Do you shut down and avoid, do you become angry and yell, or do you escape through TV, books, work, drugs, alcohol or other diversions?

3. Not every issue in your life can be dealt with at the same time. Spend some time thinking about what one thing or area in your life you would like to process more deeply with God as you continue reading this book. Focus on that issue as you work through the principles presented. Be prepared to switch to another issue should God prompt you to move into another area of your life.

STARTER PRAYER

Father God,

Thank you for pouring your love into my heart. Help me understand myself better so I can receive that love more fully. I admit I sometimes feel lost, lonely, and distant from you but I truly want to know you more intimately. Reveal any issues buried deep in my heart preventing me from experiencing your love. Prepare my heart for the truth, and strengthen me so I can deal with that truth. Encourage and support me as I walk through this process so I can be set free to enjoy the abundant life you offer me in Christ.

To you be the glory,
Amen

Chapter 2

TWISTED ROOTS

But the LORD God called to the man,
"Where are you?" He answered,
"I heard you in the garden, and I was afraid because
I was naked; so I hid."

—Genesis 3:9-10

IT'S NOT MY fault!" Pleading my case to my father, the blood dripping down my left ankle made it difficult to conceal the fact that I had cut myself on the broken vase he was holding in his hand. "It was an accident! I fell off the bed!" My father didn't buy it. He kept probing me with questions until I gave up and confessed. "OK, OK. I was jumping on your bed and didn't see the vase on the floor. When I jumped off the bed I landed square on the vase."

When I was a little girl, I saw my parents' bed as the biggest and best bed in the house to jump on. But one of our family rules was "no jumping on beds," especially our parents' bed. I broke that rule more often than I can remember and got myself into quite a bit of trouble. It didn't seem to matter, though. I loved to jump and didn't want to stop. Even though I was young, sinful attitudes in my heart were quite visible.

Humanity has been tainted by sin. In their innocence, children communicate the effects of sin quite vividly. Just walk into any elementary school and you will see selfishness, teasing, manipulative whining, social cliques, and rebellion. Children haven't learned how to hide the affects of sin yet, which is why they so visibly display it. As we grow, we learn self-control and appropriate behaviors. These things in and of themselves don't mean we have stopped sinning, just that we have learned how to hide the external visibility of our sinful nature.

Because we learn how to behave appropriately as we grow, we forget that our hearts have been tainted by sin. Our failure to grasp the cost of sin in our personal lives causes us to fail to appreciate the gift of grace and salvation given us from God. What I am trying to say is that when we fail to recognize how deeply our personal sin attitudes and behaviors affect us, we fail to acknowledge the damage they create in our lives and in the lives of others. This failure blinds us to the truth. Because we don't see the truth, we don't grasp the full impact of what God has saved us from. If we don't know what God has saved us from, how can we truly appreciate what Christ did for us on the cross?

Ask anyone who has been severely broken and restored to share his or her appreciation for God. These people know what God has saved them from and that knowledge helps them live passionately for him. If we want to grow spiritually deep, then we need to grasp the full extent of what God has saved us from. Without this understanding, we risk becoming like the Pharisee Jesus described in one of his parables. In the parable, a Pharisee thanked God that he was not like evildoers, adulterers, or tax collectors (Luke 18:9-14). In other words, he believed himself to be more religious than the rest, but in reality, he was spiritually dead. We don't want our spirituality to be full of hollow words;

we want it to be passionate and full of meaning. In order to get this passion and meaning, we must consider how the fall altered the condition of our hearts.

THE FALL OF MANKIND

When reading the Bible we often view the people in the stories as two-dimensional characters void of any real personality or feeling. We forget the stories come from real people who made real, often difficult, decisions. Their stories depict how their decisions impacted their circumstances and the circumstances of those around them. Adam and Eve's story is the most tragic. More than any other event in history, the impact from their decision set in motion the most damaging consequences to all of creation. When they ate from the forbidden tree, they literally changed the future of mankind.

Contemplate Eden for a moment. Imagine beauty in its purest form. In Eden, every bush, plant, or blade of grass adorned the grounds with spectacular brilliance. The multitude of plant and animal life engulfed the senses with sights, sounds, and aromas beyond anything we can ever imagine. Every breeze moving through the trees would generate a sweet sound of heavenly praise to our beloved Creator. Just imagine a place where every created thing was perfect and showered peace and tranquility upon the heart. Adam and Eve lived in such a place. They tasted life in its flawless magnificence. Everywhere they went, they were engulfed in absolute splendor.

Not only did they exist in beauty, they themselves were pure in heart and soul. They were delighted to discover feelings of laughter, happiness, and love. They were captivated by a perfect marriage as they shared pure intimate love for one another (Gen. 2:21-25). Their joy was made complete through their spiritual connection with God. Theirs was a connection with God unlike anything we can ever have this side of heaven. You see, prior to the fall, sin did not interfere with Adam and Eve's spiritual relationship with God. This gave them the benefit of experiencing a totally pure, healthy, emotionally secure love with our beloved Creator. Being firmly grounded in his love also gave them a strong confident sense of self. Together, they were to cultivate the earth and make it a thriving environment for all humanity (Gen. 1:28). Initially, theirs was a world that had everything they could ever possibly need, completely perfect in every way.

Then one dreadful day, they were tempted by Satan and came face to face with an enemy for which they had no experience. They came face to face with *the sinful desires of their flesh*. God gave mankind the freedom to choose to obey. Complete freedom always comes with a choice—to obey or not to obey. If we don't have the option to refuse obedience, then our freedom to respond to God's love is not authentic. It's artificial. We would be puppets under God's control, and God does not want puppets. He desires that we willingly choose obedience. This is why we have the choice to reject God's righteous ways.

On that day in paradise, Adam and Eve were caught between two choices. Should they obey God's command, or should they exercise their freedom to rebel at the restrictions? As Eve was tantalized through conversation with the serpent, Adam became enticed quietly within the confines of his own mind. Both, however, came to the same conclusion: what they had been given was not enough, and they were *entitled* to more. Then with just one bite–WHOOSH! It was all over. Perfection was gone.

THE IMPACT OF THE FALL

Did you feel pain in your heart over those three little words as I did in writing them? Perfection was gone! In an instant, everything in Adam and Eve's world changed. All that was perfect was now twisted. Scripture says that immediately their eyes were opened and they knew they were naked (Gen. 3:7). This means that at the very moment they put the fruit into their mouths, their consciences flared into being.

Our consciences are the internal moral gauges in our hearts that inherently inform us of what is morally right or wrong. Prior to the fall, Adam and Eve had not felt the damaging effects from their consciences indicating a wrong behavior. They must have been overwhelmed with the onslaught of emotion that came upon them the moment they sinned. One thing is certain: because Adam and Eve were obedient to God prior to the fall, they were not accustomed to dealing with the negative emotions suddenly surging through their hearts. Interestingly, the first thing they noticed was their own nakedness. This suggests that the birth of sin immediately went to work multiplying, dividing, and distorting its negative effects, spreading like cancer in their hearts. When they looked at one another, they felt a sense of sensuality, something they never experienced before. The purity of their relationship suddenly took a different form, and they felt the need to cover up.

Adding to the weight of their action, Adam and Eve must have felt the immediate severing of their spiritual ties to God. It must have felt as if they were unexpectedly ripped away from the peace and tranquility to which they were accustomed. They probably felt disoriented and alone for the first time in their lives. Though they may not have been able to grasp all that had happened, they certainly must have felt the dizzying effects of the fall taking place all around them. In one dramatic swoop, Adam and Eve, who once walked in line with God, now stood in opposition to him. Instinctively, they must have felt that burden.

BIRTH OF THE BROKEN HEART

Immediately, we see the effects of brokenness upon the hearts of Adam and Eve. The Bible story itself describes the impact of the wounds that were inflicted. Upon hearing God in the garden, Adam and Eve hid (Gen. 3:8-10). They hid! They had never hidden from God before, but now they felt a need for protection. When confronted, Adam's reason was that *he was afraid because he was naked* (Gen. 3:10). His sense of security and confidence, formerly grounded in God's love, suddenly shifted into shame, guilt, fear, and impurity. At the core of his being, he no longer felt safe, confident, and secure. The twisting effect of sin made a home in his heart.

Because of this, Adam and Eve now experienced insecurity and a need to self-protect. Rather than seek God for help, they quickly initiated their own strength and abilities. They covered up, hid, blamed, and avoided responsibility.

In other words, their disobedience caught them unprepared to handle the emptiness birthed within their hearts. They immediately tried to fill that void with their own means of protection. Their determination to resolve the crisis on their own proved that sin had permanently changed the condition of their hearts.

All those born from them would be born with this new damaged heart condition. For this reason, all of humanity is now tainted by sin deep within and suffers the same unsettled need for protection, love, and security. Just as hair color and eye color are passed down, so is the sin-filled heart, creating our need for a savior.

These are our spiritual roots. The more we ponder this event, the greater we understand God's sacrifice and his unfathomable love. The more we grasp the nature of our hearts, the easier we comprehend that sin is not something that comes upon us; it is something inherent within us. Perhaps this example will help: a healthy baby is born with the necessary equipment needed to walk, i.e. legs and feet, but must wait until he or she physically develops appropriate muscle and brain activity in order to walk. Sin is something that is part of the condition of the post-fall human heart. As babies grow, sinful attitudes develop and express themselves externally as we experience different circumstances in life.

Overall, sin has twisted humanity's perspective of life. Now centuries past the fall, mankind has placed humanity at the center of the Universe. Post-fall humanity is terribly concerned with personal desires and selfish needs. A wide variety of self-centered attitudes have been nurtured over the years since the fall, and we need our blinders removed so we can see them.

I have listed some of the more prevalent issues in order to help shed light on self-centered attitudes fostered in the hearts of fallen man. As you read this list, you may feel something wrestling within you. If you do, stop and process your feelings with God. Ask God if he is speaking to you personally regarding a specific topic. Any wrestling in your heart should not bring condemnation; condemnation comes from self or from the enemy. God reveals truth to heal, strengthen, and perfect us in his image.

THE POST FALL SELF-CENTERED HEART

- **Man Now Needs Modesty:** At the fall, a feeling of sensuality was released in the hearts of Adam and Eve. They no longer looked at the beauty of each other's body with purity. Their thoughts toward one another possibly produced urges in their bodies that caused embarrassment and explains their need to cover up. Perhaps the intensity of our immoral thoughts is the reason behind the Old Testament laws directed against seeing the nakedness of another outside of marriage (Lev. 18, 20). Since the fall, we need protection from immorality because our hearts and minds can't handle our sexuality. When exposed to forms of sexuality, our minds create imagery and fantasy that produce lust in our hearts and entice us to act out in damaging ways. King David's sin with Bathsheba illustrates the force behind our thoughts. David was so deeply mesmerized with Bathsheba's body that her image monopolized his thoughts. It wasn't long before he acted on his desires and committed adultery with her (2 Sam. 11). Both men and women struggle against the damaging effects of immorality today. Sex has become a lucrative industry. The longer we entertain impure thoughts, and accept immorality, the harder our hearts become. Eventually, we begin to view men and women as objects of pleasure, rather than beautiful beings created in the image of God. Modesty is a gift from our subconscious minds that protects our hearts from the damaging effects of immorality. We must make every effort to protect ourselves from what we see and how much we see, because if we don't, our minds' ability to protect us through a sense of modesty will be destroyed and our hearts will harden. Jesus said that if a man looks at a women lustfully, then he has already committed adultery with her in his heart (Matt. 5:28). This is a very strong statement, illustrating the damage that takes place in the heart when our minds contemplate unhealthy sexual thoughts. When the heart suffers, the body and mind also suffer, creating immense destruction in our lives and in the lives of others. If pornography is an area of personal struggle for you, spend extended time in prayer asking God to soften your heart and cleanse your mind from its damaging effects. Find a good counselor or Christian program to help you break this addiction.

- **Man Began to Blame Others and Shirk Responsibility:** Adam and Eve became more concerned for themselves than for each other. When confronted by God, they failed to take responsibility for their own actions and they failed to protect each other. In an effort to self-protect, they blamed each other. Ultimately, Adam blamed God along with Eve while Eve blamed the serpent (Gen. 3:11-13). Neither confessed nor asked forgiveness.

We run from the truth because the truth often shines a spotlight on our sinful behaviors, and no one wants to be that exposed. Therefore, blame becomes our ally and it is an easier path to take. We blame our environment, our circumstances, our home life, our spouse, our disabilities, our ignorance, our bodies, our education, our finances, and much more. We point to whatever we find nearby and blame that as an excuse for our action or lack of action. A wife may use a disagreement in her marriage and blame her husband as a reason for divorce. A couple may point to low finances and blame a poor-paying job as reason for a failure to tithe. A boy may criticize his intelligence and blame that for his low grades. The truth is that the first couple may need counseling, the second may need to learn budgeting, and the boy may need a tutor or better study habits. The truth involves taking action and putting forth effort. Perhaps that is why we hate it so much.

God calls us to take responsibility for our actions (or lack of action) because the choices we make affect our lives and the lives of others around us. The truth can be hard to swallow, especially when having to do something we don't want to do, but when exercised, truth will set our hearts free.

- **Man Lost the Ability to Love Unconditionally:** Hopelessly self-centered, man now tries to satisfy his own need for love rather than give his love freely to others. Love is now conditional upon a need to receive something in return—hence the term "conditional love." Conditional love interferes with intimacy and relationships because it puts the needs for self before the needs of others.

In a conversation I had with a woman, she talked about keeping an accounting list to record favors done for people. Any time she helped someone she jotted his or her name on the list. When she needed help, she pulled out her booklet and expected help from the people listed. If someone failed to help when requested, this woman became angry and vowed never to help that person again. Her love toward others was conditional upon what she could receive in return. Now not many of us go to the extent of writing out a list, but we do entertain these thoughts in our minds. Have you ever grumbled that you do all the work or that you always give to others and no one ever gives to you? How about thoughts like, *I make the coffee every morning and no one appreciates what I do*, or, *I help Todd at work all the time but he never helps me*. These thoughts demonstrate conditional love. Our help, service, or loving acts become conditional when we *expect* to get something in return. We cannot help ourselves. We wrestle with conditional love in our hearts all the time.

Conditional love explains why we need to receive God's love first. We can only love him after we first feel loved by him (1 John 4:7-14, 19). He understands our brokenness, which is why he continually and *unconditionally* draws us out and pours his love into our hearts. Once we taste his love and experience him, we have the opportunity to respond to his love by opening up our brokenness to him. As we begin to drink God's love deeply, healing takes place and we are transformed. His love strengthens us. When we feel loved, we become passionate about our lover. Our passion for God becomes visible as we grow spiritually mature. When God satisfies our need to feel loved, we are set free to love others more authentically and less conditionally.

- **Man's Emotions Began to Control Thinking and Behaviors:** Not only do our emotions emit joy, love, and excitement, they also trigger our brokenness. Every time we experience difficult circumstances, our emotions trigger feelings of anxiety, fear, and pain. Some of these feelings are associated with past experiences in our hearts and they cause us to feel insecure—more insecure than we should feel. Subconsciously, we respond to our emotions by attempting to prevent ourselves from feeling vulnerable. Basically, we attempt to fix or control our circumstances, believe lies about ourselves, distort our thinking, and act out in a self-protective manner. Bottom line: we need to learn to control our emotions and not allow them to control our lives. Our emotions and self-protective behaviors will be discussed in greater detail in chapters 4 and 5.

- **Man Began to Feel Entitled:** Entitlement is an attitude concealed so deep in our hearts it can be difficult to identify. The word "entitlement" conveys the belief that we deserve to have what we want, when we want it. In other words, we claim the right to have whatever we desire and we believe that everyone must placate our demands. You see, entitlement has a twin called "expectation." When we feel entitled to have what we want, we expect everyone around us to fulfill our desires. Entitlement haunts humanity more today than ever before and Christians are just as guilty of expressing it as our non-believing counterparts. Adam and Eve demonstrated this attitude in their conversation with the serpent. All of a sudden, they believed the restriction to the forbidden fruit blocked what they were entitled to have—that is, godlike powers. Entitlement is an attitude that elevates man, putting him at the center of all creation. Entitlement says, "I am entitled to be happy, healthy, wealthy, and successful." Entitlement defines what success looks like and how it should be acquired. Entitlement bases the focus of worship on "what God can do for me" rather than "how I can worship God." Entitlement refuses to acknowledge brokenness because to do so would mean facing the truth and giving up what we believe we are entitled to have. Entitlement often creeps out of the heart concealed under the façade of Christian love. In other words, those who feel entitled choose to live out their Christian lives on their own terms by controlling what they are willing to do for God and how they will do it.

I struggle with entitlement. I wrestle within my heart all the time over what I feel God is asking me to do and what I really want to do. We struggle with entitlement corporately as well. A church community can feel entitled to grow in a direction where they feel most comfortable. One of the ways we do this is through church size. I have heard so many people speak against large church communities. I too can be overwhelmed when in a large church, but I realize we live in overpopulated neighborhoods. It would stand to reason then that our overcrowded conditions would naturally build larger churches, especially if a church is focused on saving the lost. If we truly want to love the lost, then we must learn to trust God with our church growth. Smaller towns naturally build smaller churches, while larger metropolitan areas have larger populations that potentially could build larger churches. My choice to have a community remain small is a choice of comfort and self-protection. I am not entitled to have that comfort, especially if I want to release myself to become all I can be for God. When we act on feelings of entitlement in a church-sized situation, we create an unloving environment that often discourages seriously broken people and sets us up to pick and choose who is good enough to belong to our quaint little community. Our attitudes can close a church door to the very people God has called us to reach. If we don't make the effort to fight against our self-protections, our default nature will cause us to zero in on our own desires and enable an attitude of entitlement.

- **Man Became Insecure:** Adam felt guilt, shame, modesty, and fear. His secure and confident stance prior to the fall shifted into a mess of uncertainty and insecurity. Humanity now struggles with insecurity deep in the core of our being. We face insecurity in our home when we question whether or not we are truly loved. We face it on the job when employers discuss our work performance. In fact, we face a multitude of different insecurities throughout every stage of life. Insecurity troubles us because we struggle with our identity—the concept that tells us *who we are*. When our identity is unshakable, our confidence and security will also be unshakable. For this reason, we must remember who we are in Christ. In other words, when we forget that we are special beings created in the image of God and redeemed by the love of God, we lose our identity. When we forget these things or misunderstand what it means to be *in Christ*, we find our security by assuming a false identity. We may identify with our position in the world, our jobs, spouses, education, schools, finances, successes, and beauty. This false identity causes us to adapt cultural definitions of success as markers that indicate our self-worth. When our security is tied to a false identity and tragedy hits (such as a lost job, car accident, death, or divorce), we are left devastated because we lose our identity. If we are to feel secure and experience joy in the midst of turmoil, we must have our identity grounded in Christ alone.

- **Relationships Became Hard Work:** After the fall, man's need of self-protection gave rise to a need for independence and control. I don't mean the necessary independence sought from tyrannical governments, but the individual freedom to control one's own destiny, circumstances, and relationships. We hate the thought of being controlled or under the control of another. This is why we struggle so much with the word "submit." We don't want to submit to another because we fear it will destroy our independence and ability to protect ourselves. In our quest for control, we end up building invisible, impenetrable walls between us and other people. Many such walls have been erected between husband and wife, parents and children, and brothers and sisters. These walls keep relationships at a superficial level while developing all sorts of pain and loneliness. Though we hate the void and emptiness we feel inside, we fear opening up and tearing down our protective walls.

Being relational takes a lot of hard work because it means we have to sacrifice personal desires. God, however, designed us to be relational beings. That means we were created to open up our hearts and share our lives with him and with one another—no matter what the cost. When we don't open up to God, we miss the opportunity to be intimate with him, causing us to dabble with a shallow faith. Everything in the world today must be maintained with hard work, and that includes our jobs, homes, yards, *and relationships.*

Self-confidence and security develop out of an intimate relationship with God. Our hunger for independence will compete with our need for intimacy with God. This struggle alone may be the greatest battle we face in the quest for spiritual maturity.

These are but a few of the attitudes that have formed in the heart of fallen man. These attitudes submerge so deep within our hearts that we grow accustomed to them, leaving us unaware of how they shape our lives. They become blind spots that negatively influence our decision-making process. Unfortunately, these blind spots keep our hearts hard and prevent us from hearing God's voice. If we are willing to hear the truth, the Holy Spirit will be our guide. When we honestly ask to understand our hearts, Jesus gladly answers our prayers because he knows that truth sets us free, and he desires us to live free (John 14:14, 17; 15:16; 16:23). I encourage you to prayerfully consider the post-fall, self-centered list of attitudes outlined above. Keep in mind not every issue was mentioned. Many other attitudes like pride, arrogance, and rebelliousness are nestled in our hearts as well. Pray and ask the Holy Spirit to reveal any attitudes shaping your heart. The truth may be painful for a time, but acknowledging it purifies our hearts and fills our souls with love and gratefulness for God's grace.

"FALLOUT" ON THE WORLD

Our spirituality is affected by more than our inherent sin. The event of the fall affected every created thing. Nothing was left untouched. We must not deny the fact that our broken world also contributes pain to our hearts. Every society we encounter is made up of broken individuals. The job of ruling and subduing the earth gave rise to broken, unjust rulers. Our beautiful environment fractured and is now flooded with weeds. The process of gathering food requires heavy labor (even though most of us don't labor at gathering food today, the difficulties experienced in the workplace equal the hard food-gathering labor previously faced). The perfect weather systems God created shifted, causing natural disasters. These disasters have intensified over time and are currently reaching devastating proportions. Multiple forms of sickness, disease, deformities, abnormalities, and birth defects have also increased exponentially since the fall. In fact, the apostle Paul describes the whole of creation as, "Suffering under the pains of childbirth longing to be set free from the bondage of slavery to corruption" (Rom. 8:20-22). This bondage of slavery to corruption includes things like slavery, discrimination, tyranny, civil corruption, national corruption, environmental corruption, employer/employee abuse, animal abuse, child abuse, spousal abuse, and every other evil thing one can imagine.

History also demonstrates that the hearts of each subsequent generation of people hardens a little bit more than the generation before it. This is most evidently seen in the movement of culture and society away from godly values and principles. Remember, the harder the heart, the harder it is to hear and understand the ways of God.

Current culture exists so far removed from the fall that the fallout from sin has multiplied and duplicated itself to such a degree that the whole of creation has degraded well beyond measure. This is why illnesses like cancer are so prevalent and natural disasters so powerful. Paraphrasing Paul, our generation is like a woman in labor whose contractions are becoming more intense and frequent. Though we may deny or find ways to numb the pain, we cannot avoid the contractions. Whether we are conscious of it or not, we feel the weight of every display of corruption, natural disaster, health scare, and act of terrorism. However, we must not give up hope. We must not allow the fallout of sin in the world to corrupt our hearts with sinful attitudes. Every generation has faced difficulties unique to its culture and society. God did not abandon them, and he is not about to abandon us.

SUMMING IT ALL UP

Our perceptions of our spirituality have been molded by our spiritual roots. The twisting of sin within our hearts has permanently altered our vision. Because of inherent sin, humanity has shifted its focus to the protective needs of self. In other words, man's self-centeredness has given rise to a need for self-protection and self-preservation, coercing us to look inward toward personal needs rather than outward toward the needs of others. Attitudes associated with our spiritual roots form deceptive blind spots in our hearts that are difficult to identify. We unconsciously display these attitudes in our effort to feel safe, secure, and loved. The longer we entertain these attitudes, the harder our hearts become, affecting our ability to worship God wholeheartedly. We end up worshiping God on our terms rather than seeking his will for our lives and our church communities. This causes us to crave entertainment and comfort over discipleship and spiritual formation.

If we don't take the time to reflect upon the outcome of the fall and its influence upon our lives, we end up dangling in the shallow end of our spirituality and grow fearful of the world. To put it plainly, we fail to grow spiritually strong. Furthermore, we become enslaved to our sinful attitudes because they contribute to our decision-making processes. If we want to make a positive impact for the kingdom of God, we must learn to endure corruption in the world without fear and consider attitudes in our hearts that interfere with our ability to hear God's voice.

God can reveal the true desires of our hearts. Prayer plays an essential part in receiving his truth. We must not only pray for the truth, but must be willing to accept the truth. Meaning that as we pray for God to reveal the motivations of our hearts, we must also be ready and willing to confront whatever we discover. David understood this point well when he wrote, "Search me, O God, and know my heart; test me and know my anxious thoughts. See if there is any offensive way in me, and lead me in the way everlasting" (Ps. 139:23-24).

To walk free with the Spirit, we must be ready to see the ugliness in our own hearts. We must be prepared to confront any negative attitudes taking up space within us. The more we become self-aware and dependent upon God, the more victorious we become in Christ.

REFLECTIVE THOUGHT

1. Reflect upon the concept of the fall and our broken hearts. Did any particular area listed speak to you personally? In what ways did you identify with that topic?

2. Think about the world today. How has our current decline in morality and sound ethics affected the way you interact with people? Do you react differently to different groups of people, for example: neighbors, friends, co-workers, family, church family? Pray and ask God to reveal attitudes in your heart that contribute to your perspective on current events and social gatherings. For example, the decline in the world may produce anger, frustration, or fears. Ask for the root cause of any of these emotions and pray for God to help you understand and confront your discoveries.

3. Meditate upon Psalm 139:23-24. Pray that God would reveal any ways in your heart that are hindering your spiritual growth. Pray for the strength to confront the truth and for the courage to make significant changes.

STARTER PRAYER

Father God,

You are holy and righteous and there is none other like you! Please help me understand the depth of sin that has affected fallen man and the whole of creation. Help me understand the ways I have been influenced by inherent sin attitudes in my heart. Reveal any negative attitudes in me that are causing me to react in a self-protective manner and preventing me from growing spiritually deep. Help me battle those attitudes and trust you always for my well-being. Please, cleanse my heart and release my spirit to walk freely with your Spirit. Teach me your ways and guide me in your truth so I can become all that I can for you.

In Jesus' name,
Amen

Chapter 3

BROKEN TWIGS

When a train goes through a tunnel and it gets dark,
you don't throw away the ticket and jump off.
You sit still and trust the engineer.

—Corrie Ten Boom

WHENEVER I THINK about my yard, I envision something mesmerizing and full of color. Perhaps my mind is drawn to that imagery because so many paintings present beautiful gardens as places of peace and tranquility—something I find desirable.

As you might have guessed, the more time I spent contemplating beautiful gardens, the more I wanted to transform my yard into something gorgeous. All it really needed was some light weeding and a little planting, or so I thought. Well, truth be known, my yard was in need of a lot of weeding and a lot of planting. I've come to accept the fact that in the Pacific Northwest the rain not only cultivates beautiful trees and multicolored flowers but also a wide variety of weeds. One such weed, the perennial clover, seemed to have declared war against my lawn. The roots of this weed grow runners underground that spread out in every direction. They can be extremely difficult, if not impossible, to eradicate, and my yard was full of them.

One spring morning, after having a rather wearisome disagreement with my husband, I decided to go outside and clear a section of my yard that was overrun with these weeds. I was full of anger and thought that pulling the weeds would not only prepare that section for flowers, but also allow me to work out my frustrations. I equipped myself with a hoe and a shovel and the determination to put every bit of my energy into digging deep into the soil.

As I worked, my body passed through several different stages of agony. My back ached with every throw of the hoe as I cut into the hard soil. Blisters formed on the palms of my hands. My heart pounded heavily in my chest, but I would not yield until the section had been cleared. Several hours later, the weeds were gone and so was my anger.

I finally began to talk to God, who very gently drew me close and comforted me with his presence. I felt him tell me that my heart was just like my yard, full of messy weeds. During that time in my life, I was full of anger, bitterness, and unresolved pain. God knew I needed help, but in order for me to see that I needed help, he had to tell me the truth. After revealing the messy condition of my heart, God gently told me to put forth the same energy and determination I had used cleaning up my yard into cleaning up my heart. You see, God wanted to transform my life into something beautiful just as much as I wanted to transform my yard into something beautiful. And God chose that day, the day I was painfully clearing weeds in my yard, to reveal the true condition of my heart. God uses all of creation to teach us his principles. He will speak to us, but we must be ready to *listen,* and be *willing* to hear what he has to say.

God told me that I was in need of the Master Gardner because my heart needed tending. In other words, I had to start dealing with the issues clogging up my heart. When I was outside pulling weeds in my yard, I dug deep into the soil so I could reach the root of the plant in order to remove it completely. If I focused solely on the surface portion of the weed, the root underneath would spread out and grow again in the same place or someplace else in my yard. The same is true concerning our personal lives. If we deal solely with the surface issue causing our discomfort, we temporarily fix the problem, but leave the root issue free to resurface again and again. We end up exhausted, "fixing" the same problems over and over.

When we try to avoid any real pain or discomfort in life, we exert tremendous effort fulfilling that objective. Our efforts produce the behavioral pathways discussed in chapter 1. Basically, our desires to avoid painful issues in our lives pressure us to develop behaviors that protect our hearts from pain. Keep in mind, our spiritual self and physical self are intimately connected, so any protective desires produced in our hearts compel our bodies to behave one way or another. These self-protections keep us from feeling deep emotional pain by allowing us to temporarily feel better. Unfortunately, any time we attempt to heal ourselves apart from God, our self-protections address the surface issue only, leaving the root issue intact. Because we fail to heal successfully, we are left vulnerable to future emotional pain. The following illustration shows how this works in real life.

Doug's father left him while he was a young boy, causing a root issue from abandonment. As an adult, he suffered from broken personal relationships and difficult partnership separations. The more he engaged in personal or business relationships, the more he felt afraid of being hurt and abandoned. This fear made him work harder to please everyone around him. In a new partnership, he poured himself into the relationship, neglecting professional and personal boundaries. When this partnership ended, he was crushed and felt emotionally overwhelmed by the circumstances. From that point forward, he decided to work alone so he wouldn't be hurt anymore.

The wound produced by the abandonment of Doug's father affected his identity and sense of security. This unresolved issue in his heart left him vulnerable when interacting with people. Deep in his heart at a subconscious level he wrestled with insecurity and self-worth. Ultimately, he feared rejection and this drove him to become a people pleaser. The root issue underneath his emotional pain caused him to self-protect in a manner that gave him a false sense of security. By pleasing people he believed that he was needed and loved. Unfortunately, his pleasing behaviors failed to get the desired results. Therefore he chose a different method of self-protection, withdrawing from people all together. Doug was unaware that he was living his life and making decisions out of the brokenness of his heart.

When blinded to our root issues, we unwittingly get stuck conducting life out of our brokenness. At a subconscious level, our brokenness causes us to conceal our pain by utilizing our self-protective behaviors. These behaviors may include things like denial, lying, avoiding relationships, drinking, eating, isolation, judging ourselves or others, gossip, living in fear, and countless other behaviors. We need to discover the truth so we can expose our brokenness and seek God for deep healing and support.

The good news is that once our brokenness is exposed, it no longer has the same power of control over us as it once did because the root issue is revealed. When we know exactly where we need healing, we have a specific issue to bring before the Lord. He immediately goes to work softening the hardness of our hearts and allowing us to feel his love more fully. When we feel his love, we gain confidence, self-worth, and a sense of security. The more we experience God's love, the more we hunger for him, causing us to dive deeper into our relationship with him. Bear in mind, even with God's help, these root issues are difficult to discover. God will not reveal more than we can bear at any one time. And rarely do our issues go away overnight. Healing takes time and commitment on our part. We must learn patience and depend on God for the outcome of the process.

PERFECTING THE HEART

As we begin to contemplate our past experiences, it's important to remember that these are the areas of our life we don't want exposed. Many of us have spent decades hiding from the truth. As long as we self-protect (control and fix) and keep our painful issues hidden, we remain enslaved to our brokenness. When enslaved, the choices we make in life are determined by our self-protections rather than guided by the presence of the Holy Spirit. Fortunately for us, Jesus has set us free from the desires of our flesh (John 8:34-36). The apostle Paul pointed this out when he wrote, "It is for freedom that Christ has set us free. Stand firm, then, and do not let yourselves be burdened again by a yoke of slavery" (Gal. 5:1). When we fear truth and conceal our brokenness, we willingly remain enslaved to our flesh. That's why it is so important to remember that Christ died to set us free from sin—*all* sin. This means that he died to liberate us from the tyranny of our flesh.

Discovering the truth is the key to our freedom. Jesus said, "You will know the truth and the truth will set you free" (John 8:32). Learning the truth about our salvation is the first step we take in our Christian walk. Growing as a Christian involves learning the truth about the manner in which we are living out our Christian life.

The Holy Spirit is our guide to the truth. He reveals our deep wounds and our enslavement to specific self-protective behaviors. If we are to learn the truth about the manner in which we conduct our lives, we must prepare ourselves to see what we may not want to see—the true condition of our hearts. Once that is discovered, we can take the steps needed to break the chains that enslave us to our self-protective desires.

Truth and freedom work together. Let's look at this point another way. The apostle Paul wrote that God is busy at work perfecting us until Christ comes again (Phil. 1:6). This work began in our hearts the moment we accepted Christ as our Lord and Savior and continues within us to the day of our death. It involves purifying our hearts of sin and brokenness issues preventing us from becoming like Christ. We can fight God in this process, but there is a monumental difference in the productiveness of our earthly lives when we *choose* to work with him, rather than *fight* against him. Truth sets us free, and freedom allows us to grow.

Our willingness to accept the truth benefits us significantly. For example, it teaches us how to maneuver difficulties in life with strength, character, and a deep faith. Allowing ourselves to be perfected by God renews our minds, enabling us to pursue his will for our life without fear of where he may lead. There is something very rich and gratifying when we allow God to fertilize our soul in a manner that suits him.

Alternately, when we wrestle God and fight him every step of the way in the perfecting process, we shrink back in our faith and remain weak in both character and strength. Eventually, our rejection of truth dulls our ears to hearing God's voice. We lose the ability to discern his will for our lives and our relationship with him remains superficial. And since we don't want to face the truth, we seek God only when needing rescue from our situations.

If we call on God only when we want to be rescued from our circumstances, we are looking at him as nothing more than a genie in a bottle. We expect him to answer our demands for rescue so that we don't have to deal with any of the uncomfortable issues in our lives. When we view God this way, what happens to our faith when our circumstances don't change? Sooner or later we lose our faith.

I have heard people say things like, "I tried doing things God's way and it didn't work out for me" or "What has God ever done for me?" These statements are expressions of entitlement from individuals believing their circumstances should change miraculously with little effort on their part. If our beliefs tell us that God must make us happy, healthy, and successful, then we aren't responding to him for his love. This attitude suggests that we aren't interested in forming a relationship with him. We only want his miracles. Sadly, when adversity hits, we justify negative attitudes toward God because subconsciously we believe he did not perform according to our satisfaction.

God desires to be intimate with us. He may choose to use our pain to draw us closer to him. He may have plans for us that depend upon our experiencing some turbulent circumstance. He may want to use our situation to grow our character and develop our faith. Or he may be testing our faith as he did with Adam and Eve, using the forbidden fruit. There are several reasons why God would leave us in, or even create, difficult circumstances in our lives. Our circumstances (issues, wounds) are opportunities for our hearts to be perfected *if* we allow God to use our situations (issues, past hurts) to benefit our lives.

When we choose to avoid dealing with our issues or difficult circumstances, our faith dries up because all our energy is focused on dodging the hardship rather than drawing near to God. A desire to be free of all discomfort develops nothing but a shallow faith. We don't want a shallow faith. We want a deep spiritual connection with God. We get that connection by looking into our hearts and dealing with whatever is revealed.

The benefit of accepting the truth is feeling God's penetrating love. As God touches our hearts, the cleansing water of his immense love permeates our souls. Not only does this transform our hearts, it also sets us free from the enslaving behaviors of our flesh. The more we interact with God, the more we come to *know* his deep love in a very real and experiential way. This is the deep love the apostle Paul prayed the Ephesians would come to understand (Eph. 3:14-19).

Because of this deep love, Paul was able to continue preaching even while being tortured and living in chains. As we respond to God's love, the issues we have buried for so long lose their power over us because once we *taste* the goodness of God, our flesh no longer hungers for the false security of our self-protection, but for God alone. The psalmist describes it this way: "As the deer pants for streams of water, so my soul pants for you, O God" (Ps. 42:1).

When secure in God's love, we develop the strength needed to shed our self-protections. Then we are ready to plunge into the deep end of our spirituality and release ourselves to fearlessly become all we can be for Jesus. It all starts with a willingness to look into the messiness of our own hearts with God.

Issues of the Heart

I realize I am asking you to open up some pretty old wounds. After years of exhausting work keeping a lid on your pain, I am now telling you to let it go. Release your hold, take a deep breath, and look inside. This look, in and of itself, can leave you rather unsettled, anxious, filled with tears, and emotionally drained for a time. But rest assured, God will be with you every step of the way. When Jesus said that he would be with us always, he meant it (Matt. 28:20). If you have accepted Christ to be your Lord and Savior then you are *in Christ*. This means that we are in him and he is in us. We cannot be separated from Christ no matter what we do. Trust him to walk with you throughout this process.

In order to understand our protective behaviors, we first need to understand the depth of our brokenness. In his book *Inside Out*, Dr. Larry Crabb discusses brokenness and self-protection in great detail. He writes, "We can't recognize self-protection until we see what we're protecting. Until we face our disappointment as a victim, we cannot clearly identify the strategies we've adopted to insulate ourself from further disappointment."[2] The point of looking into our past experiences is to learn how our deep emotional pain increased our need for self-protection. The purpose is to reveal the truth behind our protective behavioral pathways, not to point a finger, blame, or increase the bitterness of our hearts over past circumstances. We want to heal successfully. That means we must look at the events that spilled harmful consequences into our hearts, causing our need to self-protect.

Bearing the burden of another's sin, especially from a loved one, is the most common way our root issues end up so deep in our hearts. Even though we deserve to be treated fairly in life, we are not guaranteed to receive fair treatment. As chapter 2 clearly points out, the fall radically changed the conditions of both humanity and our world. Every family is made up of broken individuals. Unfortunately, some are more broken than others. Do not be deceived into believing that your family is not broken just because it appears healthy and happy. There are only degrees of brokenness that separate one family from another. Keep in mind that some of our brethren have endured circumstances caused by individuals far more broken than others, making their pain far more extreme.

Another point to consider is that our self-protective behaviors spill harmful consequences onto those with whom *we* come in contact. We unwittingly do to others what has been done to us. Sin issues and protective cycles move from generation to generation and spread out just like the weeds in my yard. This is why we cannot afford to neglect the weeds in our hearts. We have the responsibility to do our best to protect those we love, and we can't do that if we remain blinded to the true condition of our hearts.

One last point. A few people questioned the purpose of looking back into past issues when they felt they had already dealt with those areas of their life and had "moved on." If we don't allow God into the process of "moving on," we only deal with the surface issue and we leave the root issue intact. We "move on" under our own self-sufficiency and self-protective nature. We have the strength within us to quench the Holy Spirit and remove ourselves from any painful situation. When we claim that we have "moved on," it does not necessarily mean that we have healed. With God we have the opportunity to grieve the loss or pain and heal the wound, leaving our heart soft and receptive to his touch. After walking through this process, those who questioned it soon understood its benefit.

LOOKING INTO THE PAST

For so many of us, the starting point for our deepest wounds came through our biological roots—our early childhood experiences. Being raised in an alcoholic family, a physically abusive family, or a controlling family definitely leaves dreadful scars on the heart. Nevertheless, keep in mind that early childhood encounters are not the only source of deep wounds. Some of our scars developed from poor decisions made during our young adult years. The first years of independence combined with inexperience and immaturity often result in consequences that harden the heart. Even those who were raised in loving homes are not immune from deep wounds. Some loving families tragically overprotect their children, producing a multitude of fears and a desire to withdraw from the world.

Whatever the cause of our pain, these are the roots we desperately try to conceal. As we take an introspective look into the reality of our past experiences, we want to distinguish our feelings from our self-protective behaviors. In order to do this, we must spend some time in prayer with the Holy Spirit, contemplating our past. Ask yourself questions such as: What was life like in my childhood home? How did I get along with my parents? Was my relationship different with my mother than with my father? Did my parents divorce? How did I get along with my siblings and friends? Did my family move frequently? How did I handle life as I entered school? Am I afraid of the decline of our nation, government, the public school system, nonbelieving neighbors, my children's safety? As you ponder these questions, ask the Holy Spirit to reveal the truth behind the emotions you feel.

To help you process your past, I have listed a few common areas of brokenness coming from our families of origin. Our emotions often trigger these root issues and cause self-protective behaviors. The list is not exhaustive, but gives a few illustrations and a glimpse at some of the more painful circumstances that develop a need for self-protection. Keep an open heart and mind as God leads you during this process. Keep praying for the Holy Spirit to guide you into the truth.

- **Feelings of Abandonment:** Feelings of abandonment run deep in our society. So many people today are afflicted by one form of abandonment or another. These feelings can develop within us when we experience any form of physical abandonment such as the loss of a parent due to divorce, or death, or when we experience emotional abandonment such as the loss of emotional support and guidance during our growing years. The effects of abandonment also touch adult populations. Many Christians experience emotional abandonment when interacting with an unloving spouse, and regrettably divorce has become a common form of physical abandonment.

  Any time we experience feelings of abandonment, our core identity is shaken. We question our self-worth, our ability to be loved, and our sense of security. We grow fearful of future abandonment and rejection. Our self-protections can range anywhere from complete isolation and withdrawal to pleasing everyone around us.

  On the one hand, our wound leaves us fearful of intimacy and commitment. On the other hand, our fear of rejection develops our need to be needed. In *Struggle for Intimacy*, Janet Geringer Woititz, Ed.D writes, "Your safeguard against being abandoned is to try hard to be perfect and serve all the other person's needs...whenever anything goes wrong... when there is conflict...the fear of being abandoned takes precedence over dealing with the pertinent issues which need to be resolved."[3] In other words, our fear of being abandoned becomes more important to us than dealing with the real problems at hand. By giving in to our fears, we end up living out of our brokenness rather than trusting God with our relationships and circumstances.

We must wrap our minds around the truth that Jesus will never abandon us. Prior to his ascension to heaven, he left us this promise: "And surely I am with you always, to the very end of the age" (Matt. 28:20). When we believe this truth in our hearts, the fear of abandonment can no longer haunt us. The key is to remember that we are in Christ and he is in us. We can never be abandoned, because Christ has promised to see us through, from beginning to end.

- **Betrayal:** One of the most devastating wounds ever afflicted upon another happens through the betrayal of someone who should otherwise be a safe person in our life. When a betrayal happens in the home, either by sexual or physical abuse, the consequences are all consuming and often pass down from one generation to the next. The need to flee from constant emotional pain initiates several different self-protective behaviors. These protections are very hard to shed because they have provided a false sense of security for a very long time. A lack of trust, fear of intimacy, fear of commitment, and either sexual promiscuity or isolation become a few of the behaviors invading the heart. Outward displays of anger, self-mutilation, self-condemnation, withdrawal, fear, excessive need for control, and emotional shutdown can also add to the mix of feelings. If you have suffered from this form of betrayal, be careful that you don't remain stuck in the question of "why" it happened. That question can never be adequately answered. Just be willing to open your heart to God, grieve your wound with him, and pray for healing and restoration. I also suggest that you find a godly Christian counselor to help you process your pain.

- **Feelings of No Worth or Value:** All of our brokenness issues generate some feelings of low self-esteem. Without a doubt, acts of physical or sexual abuse erode one's identity and push the abused person to the brink of no self-worth. But emotional abuse, a very manipulative form of abuse, touches far more people. The emotional abuser wears down the victim's sense of self through emotional manipulation, abusive language, anger, nagging words, or constant belittling as a means of control. The goal is to control the thinking and actions of the other person. Being under this level of control robs us of self-confidence. Gregory L. Jantz, Ph.D. describes those with low self-esteem as habitually giving in to the desires and demands of others because they doubt their own ability to make good decisions.[4] These doubts contribute to our feelings of unworthiness. The sad truth is that when we don't see ourselves as valuable, we fail to believe that God values us. This makes us live in fear of exercising our personal rights or voicing our personal opinion. We slowly become inactive and substitute our abundant lives for one of mere existence. Yet the apostle Paul wrote, "When we were still powerless, Christ died for the ungodly....God demonstrates his own love for us in this: while we were still sinners, Christ died for us....For if, when we were God's enemies, we were reconciled to him through the death of his Son, *how much more, having been reconciled, shall we be saved through his Life!*" (Rom. 5:6-10, emphasis mine). Believe me, God values us! He gives us the strength and courage needed to make a decision, voice an opinion, and risk living once more. Regaining our sense of value heals the wounds low self-esteem leaves behind.

- **Feelings of Fear:** In the book *Kitchen Table Counseling,* the authors describe fear as a natural response to danger, either real or perceived. They rightly acknowledge fear as a God-given emotion designed for our protection. They also suggest that exaggerated fears become phobias.[5] When exaggerated fears no longer remain in the healthy, protective range, they become unhealthy issues afflicting our hearts. Fear of this magnitude is by far the most incapacitating emotion we may experience. Fear causes us to retreat, deny, lie, avoid, and remain inactive.

Many fears originate in Christian homes that accentuate an unhealthy fear of the world. This exaggerated fear causes us to self-protect through overprotection, which seriously weakens our Christian walk because it places our security in our own hands, preventing any need of God. Overprotection increases our ability to control and fix our circumstances our way. Sadly, many of us justify serving the Lord with tithes and service solely in our local churches. We play it safe and never venture out into neighboring communities needing help. Fear corrupts our ability to "love" our neighbors. We have been commanded to be in the world, but not of the world (John 17:11; Rom. 12:2).

Fear moves from generation to generation, causing Christians to shrink back from the world and live exclusively in Christian circles. Our belief in the things we fear keeps us from taking any risks or initiative to boldly step out in faith. Our inactivity produces complacency, further eroding our faith. We become like the Pharisees, who erroneously believed they had greater faith than everyone else, but in reality had hardened hearts.

Our circumstances always generate some degree of fear within us. We may fear for our children, intimacy, divorce, loss of security or finances, making a wrong decision, or people discovering the truth. However, our fears are not the problem. How we allow them to control us is.

- **Lost Trust:** Abuse, abandonment, neglect, pain, hurt, and fear predispose us to a lack of trust with God and people. Because we have adapted to so many situations of broken trust in the home, we've grown self-sufficient and we place little trust in God to supply our needs. We exercise our ability to control our circumstances because we subconsciously live in fear of being hurt, rejected, unloved, used, or abandoned all over again. When dealing with others, our lack of trust causes us to vacillate between excessive neediness and staunch independence. Authentic intimacy is lost.

  A lack of trust not only hurts our ability to relate with others in a healthy manner, it also impairs our ability to be intimate with God. Learning to trust God for our needs and relationships is essential for our spiritual growth. This entails a willingness to move in a direction away from an overprotected, secure little life to one that faces difficult challenges.

SUMMING IT ALL UP

Our biological roots set the tone for how well we maneuver difficulties in life. Our early childhood experiences place impressions upon our hearts that often increase our need of protection. As we mature, we develop the means to insulate ourselves from our emotional pain by developing self-protective behaviors that give us a false sense of security and love.

In order to heal, we must first acknowledge the truth. We must look objectively at our difficult, often painful, memories. Our memories come from moments in our lives that impacted us in either a positive or negative way. These past experiences helped shape us into the adults we have become. Positive experiences gave us confidence and self-assurance, but negative experiences crushed our self-esteem.

Our past negative circumstances are very real and must be validated. When we or others invalidate our pain, we feel the loss deep inside our hearts. One of the ways we protect ourselves from this pain is through creating lies that blind us from the truth (a form of self-protection). For example, a family may deny the damaging effects of alcoholism by believing the lie that alcohol is not the problem. Or if someone we love is depressed, we may believe we have the ability to "fix" him or her by working harder at making that person happy. The more we accept the lies, the more we invalidate the truth and our own pain. We end up stuck living life out of our brokenness rather than out of the grace of God. In other words, the more energy we exert avoiding the truth, the more entrenched we become in our brokenness. Our life becomes one of existence where spiritual growth is minimal because the hardening of our broken hearts impedes our connection with God. Being hopelessly stranded in a superficial relationship with God leaves us walking through life enslaved to our self-protections rather than devoted to Christ.

In order to heal, we must validate our pain by acknowledging the truth regarding our circumstances. Since we have no real control over the people in our life, we cannot "fix" the alcoholic, the depressed, our spouse, children, or co-workers. But we can acknowledge the truth and accept the conditions those people have placed on our lives. This means *dealing with* and *not covering up* the pain.

God already knows the truth, but when we acknowledge the truth to him by admitting that someone in our life has hurt us deeply, we open ourselves up to receive his healing touch. When we willingly ask God to help us clean up the messiness of our hearts, we place ourselves in the best possible position to be perfected by him. As I said before, there is something extremely gratifying in our hearts when we allow God to fertilize our souls in a manner pleasing to him.

REFLECTIVE THOUGHT

1. Spend time in prayer and contemplate the specific dynamics of your childhood. Ask God to reveal the truth behind any past hurts or fears that haunt you regularly. Journal your discoveries.

2. As you think about the list of wounded feelings described in this chapter, does any one area speak to you personally? If so, how does it speak to you? If you don't know, then pray and ask God to clarify your feelings. Journal any random thoughts you may have. They may clear up as you continue reading the book. The truth is not always easy to see.

3. As you think about the circumstances of your life, can you identify any specific losses you have experienced because of past hurts and fears? For example: the loss of a parent due to divorce, the loss of a fulfilling career due to fear, or the loss of self-esteem due to a poor choice in life. Open up your heart to God in prayer and begin to grieve those losses with him. Ask for specific healing to address each specific loss in your life.

STARTER PRAYER

Dear Lord Jesus,

You are holy and righteous and there is none like you. You know me intimately. You know my past, my present, my circumstances, and my pain. Only you know the true motivations of my heart and only you can reveal them to me. Remove the blinders from my eyes and reveal the truth behind my past experiences. Help me see my self-protective behaviors and help me choose to walk free of them. I admit that I fear the truth so I ask for your strength and encouragement throughout this process. Guide me toward a life lived in the reality of the truth by helping me speak the truth in love to myself as well as to others. Soften my heart with your healing touch and help me understand the width, length, height, and depth of the love you have for me.

In Your glorious name,
Amen

Chapter 4

LOST, BUT NOT ABANDONED

If your eyes are bad, your whole body will be full of darkness.
If then the light within you is darkness,
how great is that darkness! (Mt. 6:23)

—Jesus

TIM'S FATHER PACKED his bags and left home when Tim was in elementary school. His father never said goodbye and his mother never acknowledged that his father had left. All Tim knew was that his dad was gone. Two years later, his mother was involved in a new relationship with a man who had drug and alcohol addictions. It wasn't long before they moved into low income housing. As his mother catered to the needs of her new boyfriend, she neglected the needs of her son. Tim grew up in a home with no parental guidance or supportive love. He often found himself sitting alone in a dark room without any food in the house.

Pivotal moments in his life surrounded times when circumstances improved only to have his hopes crushed because the new developments soon fell apart. Overall, the wounds in his heart left him feeling as if he didn't matter—as if he had no value or worth.

Because of this, he believed he wasn't good enough to fit in with what he called "the good crowd," so he found ways to avoid those groups of people.

Unbeknownst to him, he was living his adult life out of the brokenness of his heart. Subconsciously, he conducted life as if he were a little boy sitting alone in the dark, unworthy of receiving anything good. His brokenness pressured him to remain inactive and fearful. Alcohol became his primary method of self-protection. As long as his deep emotional pain was numb, he was able to cope.

Tim's childhood experiences completely eroded his identity, security, and sense of value. As a result, his heart was full of darkness and hardened toward God. This darkness altered Tim's perspective on life and increased his need for self-protection. In other words, life became overwhelming and threatening to him and caused him to "check out."

Our ability to stand strong and make good decisions in life comes from the condition of our hearts. As our spiritual roots, personalities, and past experiences mix together, a variety of attitudes and self-protective desires are formed. These elements influence how well we see or perceive life. I believe that is the reason why Jesus said, "If then the light within you is darkness, how great is that darkness!" (Matt. 6:23). When our hearts are in the dark, our ability to understand godly ways and truths is in jeopardy. We cannot accept what we fail to see, hence the words, "Those who have ears to hear let them hear and those who have eyes to see let them see." In order to "hear" and "see" God, our hearts must be able to receive his transforming love. Living out of our brokenness prevents this from happening.

The Darkness Within

The condition of our hearts determines how well we live out our Christian life—tithing, serving, interpreting Scripture, loving others, and most importantly worshiping God. When we harbor unsettled issues or attitudes in our hearts, we respond to life with behaviors defined by our brokenness rather than guided by the Holy Spirit. The reason is that when our attitudes and past issues harden the heart, our protective desires compel us to respond to circumstances in a manner that serves us. Alternately, if the heart has been softened by God, leaving us open to the Holy Spirit, we respond to circumstances in a manner that serves God and others. For example, if a co-worker is talking harshly about another worker, do we partake, remain silent, or speak up and politely express our desire to share kind words about that worker? If a spouse seems unloving, do we divorce, have an affair, or put forth the hard work and effort needed to resolve the issue? If we receive a pay cut due to hard economic times, do we stop tithing altogether or readjust the amount we tithe? If a loved one calls while drunk demanding our attention, do we hang up the phone, spend hours in conversation, or lovingly tell that person we won't talk to him or her until he or she is sober? All of these scenarios suggest various ways we can respond to any given situation. The manner in which we choose to respond is determined by the condition of our hearts.

Our ability to make good choices in life is based upon knowledge and experience. If we avoid hardships, we circumvent a stage of human development resulting in a failure to gain experiential problem-solving knowledge. This is why our decision-making process often becomes difficult and burdensome. Sometimes we are so overwhelmed with our circumstances that we get stuck waffling back and forth between solutions. We waffle because we want to fix our circumstances in a pain-free way, and we don't know how to do that. No wonder difficulties in life leave us exhausted and fearful.

This is also why learning about our hearts is so important. The more we understand what motivates our hearts, the more self-aware we become. This helps us consciously turn away from self-protective choices and toward God-dependent choices.

Anytime we rely on our own strength to provide for our needs, the desire of our hearts persuades us to find easier ways to cope with our problems. Our need to cope amid the complexities of life is the reason we develop self-protective behaviors.

LEARNING TO COPE

Feeling loved, valued, safe, and secure is very crucial to the emotional health and wellbeing of people. When young children grow without these foundational pieces, they grow up as emotionally wounded adults filled with protective behaviors. We develop our protective behaviors when young because they help us cope with traumatic circumstances we can't otherwise handle at a young age. And it doesn't take long to learn how to adapt to a difficult situation. We may withdraw to our rooms; run away from home; deny; lie; drink; party; take drugs; excel at academics, sports, or religion; become angry with the world; or become depressed and shut down emotionally.

Here are a few examples that give us a picture of what this looks like. Becky developed a childhood protective behavior of withdrawal. Her father passed away when she was a very young girl, making her mother a single parent. Whenever her mother yelled at her siblings, the atmosphere in her home turned chaotic. Becky couldn't handle the commotion, so she withdrew to her room, climbed out her window, and sat on the roof. On the roof, she could escape the commotion inside and feel better. As an adult, Becky tries to avoid all situations involving conflict because they make her feel tense and uncomfortable. Unfortunately, her avoidance has led to many relational problems within her marriage and with her children.

Peggy developed a childhood protective behavior of denial. Peggy's childhood family developed a pattern of lying in order to keep her mother's alcoholic behavior safely under wraps. Her entire family (aunts and uncles included) partook in the illusion. Everyone ignored the main issue and scrambled to fix each situation that arose so they could continue functioning as if nothing were wrong. As an adult, Peggy felt responsible for keeping the family secret. She worked hard meeting her family's needs and forsaking her own. Denial is another common way we self-protect because it insulates us from having to face our problems.

By the time we mature, our childhood protective behaviors become the natural actions we take when emotions are triggered. In other words, they are the pathways or cycles that we travel down every time our emotions are stirred.

I like to use the illustration of riding a bike to help clarify this point. When children learn how to ride a bike, the brain develops a memory that enables the body to adapt to balance and motion. We can stop riding a bike for fifteen years, then hop on a bike and ride again because our brain has a set pathway that reminds our body how to handle balance and motion. We just know how to ride because we have mastered the skill earlier on in life, and we repeat the cycle of what we subconsciously know every time we hop on a bike.

In the same way, our brains subconsciously cycle us through the protective natures embedded in our hearts. Becky and Peggy came to realize their self-protective behaviors as they continued processing their brokenness. Becky, who climbed out her window as a child, now has to face her desire to withdraw from every conflict that comes her way. She is learning to stand her ground and deal with situations involving conflict rather than avoiding them. By dealing with her conflicts, living conditions have improved in her home. Peggy, whose family lies to keep her mother's alcoholic problem concealed, now has to face the truth and deal with her family in light of that truth. She no longer desires to partake in the family system of denial. This has put her into many challenging confrontations with family members, but God is helping her deal with her family.

At some deep unconscious level within our hearts, the issue that initiates our need to cope through self-protective behavior is grief.

We grieve the losses in our life. We grieve because we desperately need to feel loved and secure. We grieve because we are hurting and we don't know how to stop the pain.

When our wounds remain under wraps, difficult circumstances subconsciously produce grief. Just as in the example of riding a bike, our hearts cycle us through self-protective behaviors adapted since childhood. We automatically behave the same way because it worked well for us as children, and we have never learned how to behave differently.

The only way to break the destructive cycles and heal a broken heart is through bringing unconscious grief into our conscious minds. When conscious of our losses, we are free to recognize our pain for what it is: the loss of love, value, and security. When we know what needs healing and why it needs to be healed, we have a specific issue and event to bring God. When we seek God wholeheartedly, meaning with *all of our* heart, *all of our* mind, and *all of our* strength, God supplies abundant quantities of love to soften and heal our broken heart. The first step in healing is letting God into the wounded places of our hearts.

FIVE STAGES OF GRIEF

When we think of grief, we often think it occurs exclusively after the loss of a loved one. We do consciously grieve when adjusting to such a great loss. But there are other circumstances that also cause us to grieve. We grieve whenever we feel loss. More often than not, we feel our losses in the unconscious areas of our hearts where we can't always articulate our feelings. We do, however, respond to what we are feeling, whether we understand those feelings or not.

There are five different stages of grief to consider. A variety of coping or self-protecting behaviors accompany each stage. As you contemplate these stages, ask God to reveal where you may be experiencing grief as well as any specific coping behaviors you have developed to insulate you from your pain.

Denial: Humanity really hates facing the truth. We spend a tremendous amount of energy in denial. In fact, we fabricate elaborate stories and put systems in place hoping the truth will never be exposed. Denial can prompt us to withdraw from life, inhibit us from taking risks, induce addictive behaviors, and cause us to lie, spend money, and stay busy. Sadly, many believe the lie that tells us Christians don't have major problems in life. When we believe this lie, we not only deny our need for help, but ignore the issues and attitudes in our hearts that prompted our denial in the first place.

Denying the truth encourages Christians to pursue "looking good" on the outside in order to pass cultural standards of success and prosperity. This works to the detriment of our souls as they become stagnant and empty. Jesus called it "white washed tombs" (Matt. 23:27).

Furthermore, denial motivates us to justify our sinful behavior as well as others'. For example, we justify our parents' destructive behaviors when we believe we are the one at fault, aren't good enough, or need to work harder to please them. The truth may be that our parents are sinning because they have harbored deep wounds themselves and have learned to cope through protective behaviors that consequently hurt others. We justify a spouse's lack of love when we believe we don't deserve to be loved. Or when we make excuses such as our spouse is too busy doing important things to be burdened with our needs or when we claim we don't have any needs. The truth may be that our spouse is sinning by going through life with the protective need to remain distant and independent because he or she fears intimacy. Finally, we justify the excuses we make for our own poor behaviors. We are sinning when we believe the reason we were fired from a job was not our fault, when in truth we may have contributed to the situation by harboring a bad attitude and a poor work ethic.

Denial happens when families make excuses for poor behaviors in the home. Denial happens when families fail to validate the pain and hurt experienced by individual family members. Denial happens when we believe our feelings don't matter. Denial happens because we prefer to live with the curtains closed rather than open. If we remain ignorant of the problem, we don't have to face it, be responsible for it, or deal with the messiness of it. In the case of denial, ignorance is anything but bliss because denial will only perpetuate our pain and keep protective behaviors strong.

Bargaining: Unlike denial, we acknowledge that something is wrong (though we don't always know what) and we want to fix it. We try to bargain our way out of our circumstances. For example, if we need affirmation from our boss, we may tell ourselves that if we work longer hours, take on extra projects, take work home over the weekend, and maintain a good attitude, we will receive the needed affirmation. In other words, we achieve our needs through bargaining tactics. We try to make an exchange with something we have so that we can receive the results we seek.

In grief, a parent may bargain for the life of a sick child. She or he may demand that doctors run every test several times and try every medication, even experimental ones, all in the hope that something will work. Facing illness is one area where we all dabble with bargaining.

We bargain with God in our prayer life when our prayers include words like *if* you heal my child, *then* I will attend church every week; *if* I get this job, *then* I will start tithing, or *if* you fix my husband, *then* I will respect him.

Our need to fix our situations motivates us to bargain with every difficulty that comes our way. If I just keep trying. If I bring home more money. If I lose weight. If I watch more sports with my spouse. If I can just figure out how to please him/her, then he/she will love me. If I do *this* then I will get *that*. This is bargaining.

Anger: Anger is a natural emotional response. This emotion is part of the image God gave humanity. It helps us clarify what is morally right and wrong. In fact, it would be unnatural if we didn't feel angry when violated or hurt in some way. The apostle Paul said we would experience anger, but he also said we are not to sin when we are angry (Eph. 4:26). To protect ourselves from sinning when angry, we need to look into our hearts and ask God to help us understand our anger. There are several reasons why we may exhibit anger in life. For the purpose of this book, I am going to focus on anger as a self-protection in response to grief.

When we respond to major disappointments, frustrations, and failures in life with anger, then our anger can be a form of self-protection, protecting us from our fears, insecurities, and vulnerabilities. Hiding behind anger provides us the means to maintain control so we won't feel hurt anymore. We can be angry towards people because at some point in time someone hurt us, at God because we believe he left us in horrific circumstances, and at ourselves because we refuse to forgive our poor choices. Unfortunately, in our anger we can become a demanding force that negatively impacts those around us. In other words, our anger can cause us to become abusive—something to watch out for.

Anger and denial work hand in hand. As long as we don't see the truth, we can cling to our anger and feel justified.

Look at what Solomon writes about anger: "A hot-tempered man stirs up dissension" (Prov. 15:18), and "a quick-tempered man displays folly" (Prov. 14:29). I have met many people who walk through life filled with anger. It is sad but they have become so accustomed to it, they no longer recognize it as a problem.

Depression: The National Institute of Mental Health (NIMH) describes depression as an illness that involves the body, mood, and thoughts. It encompasses feelings of overwhelming sadness and despair that persist or intensify over time.[6] We all feel sad occasionally, and this is quite normal. But when our feelings of sadness dominate our everyday life and interfere with our ability to think, engage in fun activities, sleep, eat, concentrate, make decisions, value ourselves, and have hope, then we are struggling with something more than just sadness. We are struggling with depression.

There are several different categories of depression, ranging from mild to severe. The more severe forms, called depressive disorders, are valid illnesses that require treatment. Do not be ashamed if you are being treated for a depressive disorder, and do not feel guilty about taking antidepressants if they are needed. Depression is an illness.

Depression is a very real part of our culture today. It's a natural consequence of living broken in a broken and chaotic world. Most often depression hits when our circumstances are extremely overwhelming, when we experience a great loss (divorce or death), when our pleas for help go unheard, and when life somehow seems hopeless. Research determines that approximately 10 percent of the population suffers depression in any given year.[7] That is a lot of depressed people.

When depressed, we need to sort out our emotions and process our feelings in order to restore our emotional health. Dr. Timothy Foster describes a healthy emotional function as being able to admit, talk about, notice, express, and confess what we feel.[8] When depressed, those things are hard to do, therefore intervention from a good counselor or psychologist is often needed.

Acceptance: Acceptance is the final stage of the grief cycle. This is the place where we accept the truth. We recognize the pain, loss, issue, or attitude in our hearts. We no longer deny, bargain, or become angry or depressed. We accept the circumstances and are ready to deal with the problem in light of the truth.

In order to be healthy and move on with life, at some point in time we must accept the death of a loved one. In the same way, in order to walk free and grow spiritually deep, we must accept the issues in our life that have caused us pain. When we accept the situation for what it is, realizing we cannot change it or fix it, we have a chance to heal.

God offers us authentic healing. When we let God into the painful places of our hearts he guides us toward truth so that we can heal those areas causing us to grieve. Following his lead involves casting aside our self-protective behaviors and becoming completely dependent upon him for our well-being. This can be a very scary step to take, but freedom and healing come through experiencing God in a meaningful way. Saying no to our protective behaviors provides us the opportunity to build trust and dependence upon God, deepening our relationship with him. Healing becomes a wonderful byproduct of our newly deepened faith.

TIM'S STORY CONTINUED

As Tim and I talked about his childhood experiences, he recognized his need for stability (security) and a healthy, loving relationship (love/worth). He was encouraged to acknowledge the losses in his life. His losses included the lack of loving supportive parents and a healthy home life. These wounds distorted his vision and prompted him to see himself as unworthy.

For Tim to heal, he had to move through his grief and accept the circumstances of his childhood. As we worked through his wounds, a great deal of anger surfaced regarding his mother. He wasn't even aware of how much anger he had suppressed in his heart. Anger was part of Tim's grief cycle and something he needed to walk through with God. Releasing our anger with God in a constructive way is very healthy and liberating.

Moving through our grief is not easy nor is it a quick process. Tim is still working through his anger with God, but he can finally say that he feels valuable and loved. He is growing and learning to receive his identity and security in God's grace rather than from his biological parents.

Tim was challenged to step out and stand against his self-protective behaviors (which included withdrawal, drinking, and avoiding conflict). He was encouraged to pray and trust God for strength, comfort, and security during times of stress and confusion. The more he processed his pain, the more he felt loved by God. As he grew in God's love, he gained the confidence needed to move forward in life. He eventually found a good job and set some goals. Tim was being set free from the enslavement of his flesh and was growing spiritually strong through God's love.

Breaking the Self-Protective Cycle

When living out of our brokenness, whether we realize it or not, we move through denial, bargaining, anger, and depression—the first four stages of grief. Acceptance comes when we acknowledge the loss in our life that needs accepting. As long as our self-protections are in place, we may never realize our true loss and we may continue cycling through depression, anger, bargaining, and denial indefinitely.

Many of us feel a loss and describe it as an inner emptiness that can't be easily articulated. The depth of our emptiness may prompt us to believe the lie that tells us we are not good enough for that job promotion, for our parents, our spouse, our church, for____ (fill in the blank). This is why we must discern what lies beneath our emotions. If our vision is distorted, the solution to our felt losses may be to file for divorce when our marriage is unfulfilling, quit a job when our boss is intimidating, or move from church to church when feeling lonely and rejected.

Because we value happiness over suffering, we unconsciously find ways around our pain, causing us to automatically run through the stages of grief and self-protection over and over again. This is why we need God's intervention. We need his light shed into the darkness of our hearts so that we can see how our self-protections have kept us from running into his loving arms. To break free of our self-protections, we must first identify our pain and then the behaviors developed to protect ourselves from that pain.

A picture of a self-protective cycle may look something like this:

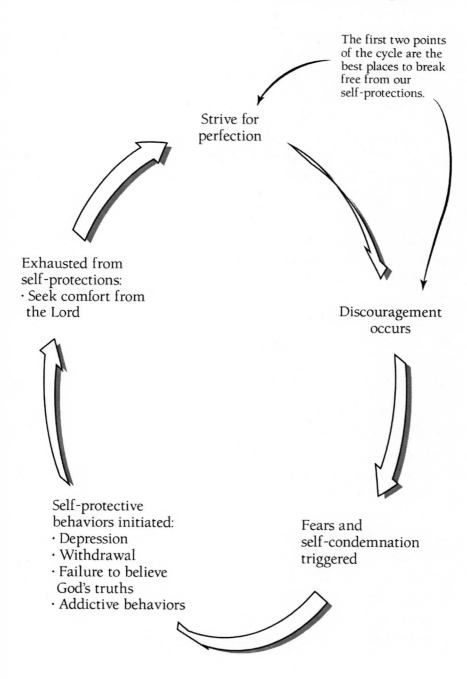

The first two points of the cycle are the best places to break free from our self-protections.

Strive for perfection

Exhausted from self-protections:
· Seek comfort from the Lord

Discouragement occurs

Self-protective behaviors initiated:
· Depression
· Withdrawal
· Failure to believe God's truths
· Addictive behaviors

Fears and self-condemnation triggered

God reveals the true condition of our hearts to help us stop blindly transitioning through this behavioral cycle. Once our trigger points are understood or revealed, we have the opportunity to heal and learn self-control with the help of the Holy Spirit. For example, when we realize that we have been striving for perfection, feeling discouraged, withdrawing from conflict, or eating when in pain, we can learn to stop the behavior. As we process our emotions and seek intervention from God the moment we feel vulnerable, we open our hearts to God for his healing touch. In order to fully break the protective cycles, we must also learn to control our thoughts and face the difficult situation. These steps will be discussed in more detail in the chapters that follow. Overall, when the heart is healed, the body naturally changes behaviors. Healing comes when we acknowledge our losses, grieve openly, and let God into the brokenness of our hearts. He enables us to walk through the pain and the uncertainties we face, free of our self-protections. Ultimately, God wants us to trust him and not our self-protections for everything we experience in life.

Summing It All Up

When protecting ourselves from difficult or painful issues in life, we generally handle our circumstances in the same manner we did during our childhood. Our childhood protective behaviors become our adult protective behaviors. These behaviors automatically go into effect the moment we feel threatened. When our past issues go unaddressed, we get stuck in our protective behaviors and end up living a life directed by our brokenness rather than guided by the Holy Spirit.

When living out of our brokenness, our past experiences, current difficulties, and our attitudes mingle together, distorting our perspective of life. A distorted perspective fills our hearts with darkness and prevents us from discerning God's light and truth. A failure to discern truth keeps us running to our protective cycles. We are left to subconsciously grieve and cycle through denial, bargaining, anger, and depression, with the hope of reaching acceptance.

Whether we face good times or bad, our hearts direct our paths so we can cope in life. Our protective cycles are addictive and unhealthy. They fail to permanently heal the wounded areas of our hearts. They contribute to our self-sufficiency and must be broken if we are to walk free.

The truth is that we cannot circumvent grief in our life. Experiencing grief and loss are part of our broken world. However, our souls can be perfected when God's love touches our tender spots, especially during times of extreme need. Truthfully, we need to be intimate with God. Intimacy with God opens up our eyes to see the world and our lives in a whole new light. Furthermore, God desires to be intimate with us. In the book of Revelation, John records Jesus saying, "Here I am! I stand at the door and knock. If anyone hears my voice and opens the door, I will come in and eat with him, and he with me" (Rev. 3:20). In this passage, Jesus is rebuking this church community because they have become completely indifferent to him. Sadly, these people grew spiritually dead because they failed to recognize their true need for Christ. The point being made is that Jesus does not want to be pushed aside because we are capable of taking care of ourselves through our own self-protective means. He wants us to recognize our need of him so that we can cling to him and he can become a vital part of our everyday lives. Jesus uses our circumstances to knock on the doors of our hearts to get our attention for the purpose of drawing us *wholeheartedly* to him. The question you need to ask yourself is this: Do you love Jesus enough to trust him with your circumstances, your pain, and your past? Will you open the door to your heart and let him in?

REFLECTIVE THOUGHT

1. Contemplate the five stages of grief. What stage or stages of grief have you experienced in the past or are currently experiencing? It might help clarify your feelings if you think about areas of tension, anxiety, or uneasiness in your life. What do you do when you experience those feelings? Run away, argue, shop, drink? Pray and ask God to help you understand what lies beneath your grief.

2. Spend some time in prayer, seeking God's clarity regarding your thinking and personal self-protective behaviors. Do you recognize any specific patterns or cyclical behaviors repeating in your life? What do these patterns look like? What practical steps can you put in place to stop the cycle? For example, if you tend to withdraw from conflict, a few steps you can take are: pray for strength and wisdom, endure the tension, express your feelings openly by speaking the truth in love, and conduct research in order to find solutions that will resolve the conflict.

3. What is Jesus using to knock on the door of your heart? Are you using a protective behavior to keep him from entering? Spend time in prayer, asking God to help you open the door to your heart and invite him in regardless of your circumstances.

STARTER PRAYER

Dear Lord,

Your love for me is as vast and deep as the ocean. When I am struggling and feeling scared, I will not be afraid for you are with me. You will never abandon me or leave me to resolve my problems on my own. You stay with me wherever I go. Father, you know where I am grieving and how deeply I hurt. Show me the pain I unconsciously try to keep hidden within my heart and help me understand it. Help me grieve my losses with you. I know you don't want me to live my life in a self-protected manner because when I do, I fail to experience your love. So reveal my self-protective behaviors and strengthen me to walk free of them. Father God, may your Holy Spirit heal the wounds deep in my heart and transform my thinking, my actions, and my life.

To you be the Glory
Amen

Chapter 5

FAITH IN ACTION

Always beware of an estimate of life which does not recognize
the fact that there is sin.

—Oswald Chambers[9]

MY BROKENNESS LEFT me insecure and my insecurities made me an overprotective parent. When my children were young, I would fanatically watch over them, believing if they were safe I would somehow be OK and able to manage life. I remember a time when a neighborhood boy (from a family who moved away long ago) played at our home when my oldest son was around three years old. He was a very active boy and a challenge to my gentle son, but my son loved to play with him. Then one afternoon my son accidentally got hurt while this young boy was visiting. After that event, I discouraged the relationship and regulated their time together so much so that the boy stopped coming over. I solemnly regret the way I handled that situation. I imagine his mother felt rejected as well because I never told her why my son could no longer play with her son. By living in my brokenness, I hurt a young boy, his mother, and my own son.

My overprotection was one of my self-protective behaviors. It wasn't until I recognized the depth of my fear and insecurities that I realized I had concealed pain. When I stepped into the truth (I cannot save my children from all harm) and acknowledged my area of vulnerability (my own fears and insecurities), I admitted to myself a need for help from God. He is the only one who can heal the wounded soul. He enabled me to release the overprotective hold I had on my children. This transformation involved work on my part. I had to learn to trust God with my children's lives and I had to learn to trust him with my life.

When we consciously know where we need help, we have a specific issue to bring before God. Seeking him with a specific need helps us grow more dependent upon him. God will help us when we seek him, but we must do our part. We must trust him and follow his lead (or his ways).

Believe me, there are moments in my life when I think standing strong and doing the right thing will destroy me. I don't like feeling vulnerable, rejected, or a failure. I detest those constant reminders that tell me I am not all that I think I am. No matter how hard I try, I cannot escape my brokenness. It always seems to emerge when I am busy looking the other way. It creeps up on me, and before I know it, I make some judgmental comment or close my eyes to a hurting soul because I don't like the external person. Sometimes I just want to escape and do whatever makes me feel better, if only for a moment. Holiness and righteousness are hard to maintain, and I cannot walk in them apart from Christ.

We are emotional beings, and sometimes our emotions tear us apart. Even though we may be convinced that God will turn everything bad into something good, life can still overwhelm us when bad things happen. Regardless of how much we know, or how hard we try, we can never be prepared for everything life will bring our way.

Never forget we are at war against our own brokenness and evil nature and the brokenness and evil nature of everyone and everything in this world. Living on this chaotic planet and interacting with its people is equivalent to living in the midst of battle. We are constantly bombarded with scattered fragments of verbal artillery shells or abusive forms of shrapnel. We inflict injury as much as we receive injury. When I feel my brokenness, it is because it has rubbed up against someone else's brokenness. When I am with someone who makes me feel vulnerable, I desperately want to self-protect so I will feel better. Make no mistake, life is pitted with one struggle after another.

Because of this ongoing battle in and around us, our brokenness forces us to stroll through life shielded by self-protection. When we don't seek help from God, by default we put all our energy into keeping protections strong and secrets hidden. This action can keep us so preoccupied with satisfying personal needs and controlling our circumstances that we become blind to the needs of those around us. We fail to love others, and in the same way, others fail to love us. Let's face it, people fall short of our expectations all the time. That is why we can't depend upon receiving our love and sense of security from people.

When we make people our only source of love and security, we either manipulate those around us to provide for our needs or become manipulated by the standards of others in order to fulfill our needs. A constant striving to meet the standards of people or worldly principles of success (wealth, health, ideal body shape, beauty, popularity, upscale neighborhoods, etc.) compels our hearts to pursue a false identity. Attempting to meet these standards increases our need of self-protection because we connect our value and worth to a person's opinion or to cultural standards and not to the love of God. When cultural standards become a ruling force in our life, our hearts persuade us to meet their demands. No wonder we are so easily devastated when our mother-in-law comes for a visit while the house is a mess or when we are not chosen for a special committee or when we are not acknowledged for our hard work.

Fictitious standards cannot determine our value and worth. Our needs for approval, love, and sense of security all come from God alone. When our needs are grounded in his love, the broken heart is transformed. This means that we must not only take on the battle going on in our hearts, but also the one raging in our minds.

LEARNING TO BATTLE OUR SELF-PROTECTIONS

When we live in the midst of our brokenness, we develop a *false dependence* on our protective natures. This false dependence leads us to believe we have control over our life and our situations. However, this dependence is really enslavement to the desires of our heart. In other words, we become enslaved to the protective needs of our hearts and believe our protective behaviors will keep things under control.

Enslavement is bondage. *Encarta Dictionary* describes it as the condition of being ruled or dominated by someone or something. When enslaved to our self-protections, we are dominated by the desire to conduct our life by our protective behaviors. Ask anyone who is addicted to alcohol, work, control, pornography, health, fitness, or success. The constant nagging drive within them is to continue feeding their need. They are not free and they are not in control. They are enslaved to the desire to continue working, eating, drinking, escaping (denying), or exercising.

It's an illusion to believe that we have any real control over our circumstances. The reality is we have no control! We don't have the power to fix the people in our life who cause us pain. We have no power to change difficult circumstances we must endure. We cannot stop an earthquake, cancer, or even the traffic jam that makes us late for work. We have no real control over our circumstances. Life just happens. But we can learn to respond to our circumstances in a way that will bring us closer to God.

When we seek God and let him touch our pain, our hearts become captivated by his love. This softens our hearts and creates a hunger within us for God because the Holy Spirit is at work pouring his love into our hearts, making us feel loved, valued, and secure! This gives us hope. The apostle Paul wrote, "Hope does not disappoint us, because God has poured out his love into our hearts by the Holy Spirit, whom he has given us" (Rom. 5:5). Hope and God's love are connected. As we grow in God's love, we open ourselves up more to God, who in turn fills us up with more love. The more we feel loved, the more hope we have in God. Hope cannot disappoint us because it is supported by God's love. This hope/love cycle is a win/win cycle that builds us up. When grounded in this love, our hope in Christ enables us to break away from our self-protections.

The bottom line is that our relationship with God is active, not passive. We need to be actively involved in the process of fortifying our faith. We must put forth the effort needed to know God intimately. Ultimately, the effort we put forth benefits us greatly by reducing our need of self-protection and increasing our faith in God.

Our faith encompasses two facets: belief and trust. These two elements work in our hearts to help us experience the fullness of God. Let's look at each of these elements individually.

BELIEF IS THE FIRST ELEMENT OF OUR FAITH

Our belief covers belief in God and his Word (the Scriptures). Our belief starts with the gospel message because God himself enables us to believe by giving us this fundamental faith. This is the work of the Holy Spirit in our hearts. But as the author of Hebrews so eloquently points out, at some time in our life we must move from milk to solid food (Heb. 5:11-14). We must grow in our beliefs.

The Bible is full of truths that teach us about God, his attributes, promises, love, sovereignty, and overall plan for humanity. These truths are life changing when we apply them to our lives. In fact, the Bible is full of stories of people whose lives were changed because of their belief in God. Chapter 11 of the book of Hebrews is often known as the "hall of faith" because it lists so many people who lived by faith. These men and women (Abraham, Sarah, Isaac, Jacob, Joseph, Moses, David, and others) followed God purely because they believed in his holiness, righteousness, and promises. In fact, their belief in God is a significant characteristic of their faith. Everyone listed in Hebrews 11 suffered traumatic circumstances in their lives, yet they refused to let their circumstances separate them from their beliefs. These men and women of faith persevered through terrible hardships because their belief was immovable. Their belief grounded them on a rock solid foundation—a foundation that gave them their identity. They knew who they were in relation to God and in relation to the world.

Our belief in God grows when we embrace who we are in relation to him as well. We are in Christ. This means that we are connected to God though Christ. Stop and think about that for a few minutes. Pretty mind boggling, isn't it?

Scripture teaches us the significance of being in Christ, and it tells us who we are (our true identity). Our true identity is not based on our job, success, spouse, education, family, culture, or finances. Those things are nothing more than functions, roles, and assets we accumulate in our earthly life. If we place our identity in any of those things, we crumble when they fall apart. For example, if someone's identity is wrapped up in his job and he loses the job, he also loses his identity—his sense of who he is. Emotional turmoil, depression, and low self-esteem can easily follow. When our identity is firmly grounded in Christ, then no matter what happens to our functions, roles, or assets, our sense of who we are will enable us to persevere. We want an unyielding identity in

Christ. In order to have this, we must build a strong foundation for it out of the truths of Scripture.

Our minds play an essential role in building this foundation. When we hear messages in our minds such as, "I am no good," "I am a failure," "I don't deserve to be loved," or "I am not good enough," we crumble because we *believe* these lies instead of believing the truths found in Scripture. All destructive messages that circulate in our minds must be stopped. We must hold these thoughts captive, and not spend any time dwelling on them. If we allow our minds to spend time on destructive messages, then our identity in Christ remains weak.

The mind and heart work hand in hand. To become strong, we not only need to heal the heart, but also to focus the mind on believing scriptural truths. In his book *Victory over the Darkness*, Neil T. Anderson emphasized this point by personalizing the plethora of true statements Scripture provides that describe who we are in Christ.[10] Read through these statements slowly starting with "I am." I am...the salt of the earth (Matt. 5:13); the light of the world (Matt. 5:14); a child of God (John 1:12); Christ's friend (John 15:15); chosen and appointed by Christ to bear his fruit (John 15:16); a joint heir with Christ sharing his inheritance (Rom. 8:17); a temple of God (1 Cor. 3:16, 6:19); a member of Christ's body (1 Cor. 12:27; Eph. 5:30); a new creation (2 Cor. 5:17); reconciled to God (2 Cor. 5:18–19); a son/daughter of God (Gal. 3:26, 28); a saint (Eph. 1:1; 1Cor. 1:2; Phil. 1:1; Col. 1:2); a member of a chosen race, a royal priesthood, a holy nation, a people for God's own possession (1 Peter 2:9-10); a fellow citizen in God's family (Eph. 2:19); righteous and holy (Eph. 4:24); chosen of God, holy and dearly loved (Col. 3:12; 1 Thess. 1:4). These truths should generate hope and build excitement in our hearts for God! If you don't feel anything after reading these truths, stop and read them again.

These statements are true statements of all who have accepted Jesus Christ as Lord and Savior. It's a lie to believe we are failures because God does not choose failures. He chooses sons and daughters who are dearly loved. Believe it! Challenge yourself to move beyond a simple belief in God to embracing the whole of Scripture as God's promise to you.

TRUST IS THE SECOND ELEMENT OF OUR FAITH

Many Christians experience tragedy after tragedy in life simply because we fail to place our trust in God. Our fears and desires to handle life our own way is behind this lack of trust. We believe that as long as we maintain control, we won't have to take a risk or challenge ourselves to endure a difficult situation. In fact, living in a culture that values happiness and comfort, many simple solutions can be justified to end our suffering.

Even though Christians disagree with culture in many ways, we still value comfort. Sadly, many of us are entrenched in it. We have indulged our desire for comfort so much that we have seriously weakened our ability to handle adversity. God's ways are difficult, and they challenge us to oppose our comforts.

The longer we walk in weakness, the greater our weakness becomes. When weak, we wrestle more intently over hardships that occur, like a lost job, divorce, rejection, finances, accidents, illness, or family disputes. When faced with opposition, weak men and women spin wildly generating emotions like anger, rage, confusion, depression, and fear. When weak, we lose patience and react quickly to our circumstances, justifying our self- protections. Self-protection provides us a quick way out, but it cannot strengthen us or build up our trust in God. Ultimately, trust and strength are built when we allow God to walk with us through hard times.

God guides us through our difficulties, but he often takes us via the path that entails hardship, fear, and uncertainty—the very places we try to avoid. Our avoidance of hardships, in essence, tells God we don't trust him with our lives. The message we send is, "Don't interfere. We know what's best for us and our families."

The truth is that we need difficulties in life to build trust in God. Adversity is a key component to our spiritual growth. Learning to trust anyone, even God, takes time, especially when we have experienced circumstances with people who have broken our trust. We need adversity to give us tangible experiences that demonstrate the faithfulness, trustworthiness, and sovereignty of God. God understands this need, which is why he not only allows us to experience hardships, but often brings hardships into our lives.

Have you ever wondered why God gave the patriarch Abraham the promise of a son, but waited twenty-five years to fulfill that promise (Gen. 12-25)? If you read through Abraham's story, you find him in the midst of several tragedies, many as a result of his own poor choices. This man faced circumstances like famine, death, marital problems, family relation difficulties, and angry neighbors. Abraham suffered one problem after another during the twenty-five years he waited for the birth of his promised son, Isaac.

But it was also during those twenty-five years that Abraham developed his unwavering faith in God. Every rescue from hardship built a stronger trust in the Lord in Abraham's heart. His ability to trust God with his life facilitated his ability to believe the promises given to him. Abraham's trust in God developed because he nurtured an intimate relationship with him. He did this by walking through each circumstance of his life worshiping, revering, and seeking God. His trust in God gave him the strength he needed to obey God's incredible command to offer his long-awaited-for son, Isaac, on the altar.

Abraham's faith assured him that Isaac would be all right because Abraham believed the promise God made pertaining to offspring and a future nation. Because of this faith, Abraham believed God would resurrect Isaac at some point after the offering (Heb. 11:17-19). Belief and trust together gave Abraham unwavering faith. This is the kind of faith we want to have in our hearts if we are to endure difficult times with peace. Our faith cannot stand on belief alone. It must be combined with trust. Trust is developed when we allow ourselves to experience adversity, and take the appropriate steps forward (no self-protection), while clinging to God.

STRENGTH IN WEAKNESS

The greatest benefit of living life in the truth is we become more self-aware. We must develop self-awareness if we are to stop living out of our brokenness and grow spiritually strong. Our brokenness is nothing more than an area of weakness within us. It's a place of vulnerability linked to situations and people. When felt, it makes us uncomfortable. We feel bad and want to fight or flee. But we don't have to let our weaknesses end with our destruction. They can become an important element that provides us the means to receive spiritual growth.

Acknowledging our brokenness reveals weaknesses in our hearts that need strength and healing from God. The apostle Paul understood human weakness all too well. Apparently, he was "timid" when speaking to the Corinthians in person (2 Cor. 10:1). Can you imagine Paul being timid? Not many of us would picture Paul that way because his writing is so powerful, yet that is how he describes himself to the Corinthians.

Paul was a man who faced many challenges during his ministry days. He faced death threats the moment he began to preach (Acts 9:23-25). He was stoned and dragged out of Iconium during his first missionary journey (Acts 14:19). He endured persecutions, suffered opposition, faced court trials, and tolerated harassment, floggings, and riots during his second missionary journey (Acts 16:22, 17:5, 13, 18:6, 12; 2 Cor. 7:5-7; 1 Thess. 2:2, 9; 2 Tim. 3:11).

He was tested by the Jews, felt deep depression, and endured beatings, imprisonments, riots, hard work, sleepless nights, hunger, and grief during his third missionary journey (Acts 20:3, 19; 1 Cor. 4:11-13, 15:32, 16:8-9; 2 Cor. 1:8-11, 2:1-2, 12-13, 6:3-13). And if all that was not enough, he preached to the Galatians while ill (Gal. 4:14-15).

Paul personally understood human weakness! He understood what it meant to be rejected, afraid, and unsure of his ability to survive a difficult situation. Yet he never stopped preaching. He never quit. He kept going strong and was dependent upon God until the end of his life. Paul knew his weaknesses, but he also knew that when we come face to face with our own shortcomings, when we stand on the threshold of collapse, and when we think we can endure no longer, *we can approach the Creator of the universe who generously gives us strength.* God not only freely gives his strength, but desires to reveal himself by doing miraculous things through our personal limitations. This is why Paul loved to boast over his weaknesses. By acknowledging his weakness, Paul was given the reason and the means to declare that his strength was furnished by Jesus Christ (2 Cor. 12:9-10).

Paul dedicated his life as a living sacrifice because he was confident in the victory that Christ won on the cross. This victory changed the way Paul viewed life! He knew that we don't become victorious by wallowing in our brokenness. Victory comes after our human frailty is covered by the strength and love of our wonderful Creator. Because of the victory won on the cross, Paul gained the confidence he needed to believe God and trust him for his wellbeing!

Paul personally experienced heart transformation, and that is why he so passionately preached the gospel. God offers us the same transforming grace he provided Paul. But in order for it to benefit us, we must believe God's Word, trust him with our lives, and grow confident in the victory of the cross.

SUMMING IT ALL UP

By living in our brokenness, we become vulnerable targets in the battles that rage on around us. We are not only consumed by our own brokenness, but also by the brokenness of everyone around us. Men and women literally move through life receiving injury from some, while imposing injury on others. As discussed in chapter 4, our hearts determine how we respond to any given situation. The desires of the heart direct our minds to follow one course of action over another. Healing and freedom come when the desires of the heart direct the mind to seek God rather than our own self-protections. When the heart develops a hunger for God alone, transformation takes place, enabling us to push aside our protective behaviors.

The heart and mind work together, but the heart has precedence. The mind understands (from experience) the pain in our hearts and that is why the mind follows the promptings of the heart. Our minds enable our bodies to fulfill the desires of our hearts by causing us to behave in a manner pleasing to the heart. No matter what our circumstances, we are always sitting between two choices. Do we retreat or stand and face our enemy? Sometimes our enemy is as simple as confronting our children, boss, or spouse. If, in our heart, we desire the comfort of peace, then nothing, not even disrespectful behaviors, will make us speak up. But if our heart's desire is to please God, then nothing will stop us from confronting a sinful behavior no matter how difficult it may be on us. The more we allow God's love to flourish in our hearts, the more our hearts will desire God, allowing us to walk free from our self-protections. The illustration found on the next page may help clarify this point.

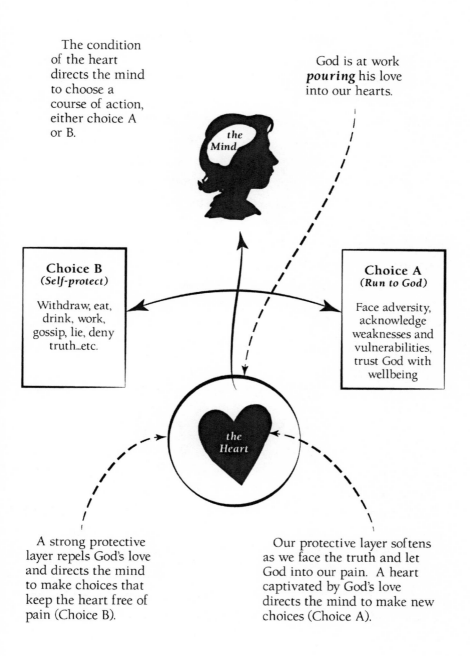

The condition of the heart directs the mind to choose a course of action, either choice A or B.

God is at work **pouring** his love into our hearts.

the Mind

Choice B
(Self-protect)

Withdraw, eat, drink, work, gossip, lie, deny truth...etc.

Choice A
(Run to God)

Face adversity, acknowledge weaknesses and vulnerabilities, trust God with wellbeing

the Heart

A strong protective layer repels God's love and directs the mind to make choices that keep the heart free of pain (Choice B).

Our protective layer softens as we face the truth and let God into our pain. A heart captivated by God's love directs the mind to make new choices (Choice A).

By acknowledging our brokenness, we develop self-awareness. Self-awareness helps us understand our fears, insecurities, and needs. Self-awareness also reveals our enslavement to false cultural standards and public opinion. As we cast aside cultural standards and seek God for our sense of security, love, and worth, we sever our ties to these false standards. Recognizing our needs gives us specific issues to bring to God. Praying for specific issues makes God real to us and contributes to our intimacy with him. The more we experience his providing for our needs, the more we grow to trust him with our life, family, marriage, children, and all that we have and are. When I realized I was overprotecting my children, I knew I had to let them go. I had to let them take some risks and fall down and get hurt. I had to let them learn to be safe and responsible through experience. And I had to trust God to protect them while they were learning. To this day, I still pray over my boys every morning as they leave for school and every night as they go to sleep. God has been incredibly faithful to me. He has never let me down, especially regarding my boys, and we have been through quite a few issues.

Our relationship with God is active, not passive. This means we have a part to play in the transformation of our hearts. Interacting with God through worship, prayer, and scripture reading helps nurture our beliefs, and we should be participating in these activities, however these activities alone are not enough to develop a deep trust in God.

To build an unwavering faith we must move beyond mere faith, and embrace scriptural truths while challenging ourselves to trust God by stepping out into a new direction with confidence. We must trust God to provide for us while we stand strong against adversity. When we compromise our values, integrity, or beliefs for the sake of our situation (jobs, marriage, relationships) we are not trusting God with our life. Trust in God is developed as we experience his faithfulness during our times of need. By refusing to self-protect or compromise and by choosing to face our difficulties with the truth, we grow phenomenally strong. This means we must let go of our desire to control our circumstances and conduct our lives with biblical principles such as honesty, integrity, responsibility, and honor.

With God's help, we can be victorious in our weaknesses just as the apostle Paul was victorious in his. Our victories start as soon as we make a conscious effort to move away from living out of our brokenness and into living out of the victory of the cross.

And he will give you all you need from day to day if you live for
him and make the Kingdom of God your primary concern.
—*Jesus* (Matt. 6:33)

REFLECTIVE THOUGHT

1. Spend some time contemplating how you see yourself. Do you identify yourself as mother, father, successful businessman/businesswoman, teacher, wife, husband, rich or poor, son or daughter? How have those titles trapped your mind into believing your identity is dependent upon those roles or functions? Ask God to help you remove any false identity markers that may be present in you.

2. The goal of walking free is to learn to be content in all things. Whether hungry or full, whether wealthy or poor, whether loved or hated, whether accepted or rejected, we are to be content in our failures as well as our successes (Phil. 4:11-13). However, destructive messages in our minds tell us we cannot be content without control or protective behaviors. Applying God's truth is the only way to overcome the desires of our hearts or the lies that resonate in our

minds. Healing and contentment come from being grounded in an identity in Christ. Review the list of identity verses listed in the chapter found under "Belief Is the First Element of Our Faith." Then look up the additional verses listed below. Read and personalize these truths. Write verses that are meaningful to you on a three-by-five card and carry them with you as an encouragement when you are feeling anxious. Journal your feelings.

John 1:12, 15:15-16; Romans 5:1, 6:22, 8:1; 1 Corinthians 3:16; Galatians 4:6-7; Ephesians 1:3-14, 2:6; Philippians 3:20, 4:6, 8-9; Colossians 1:13-14; 2 Timothy 1:7; 1 Peter 1:1-2; 1 John 3:1-2, 5:18.

3. Pray about a current situation in your life. Ask God to heal your pain and strengthen your soul to persevere. Seek his guidance and wisdom regarding your specific struggle. Step out against your desire to self-protect and trust God with your wellbeing. Be willing to acknowledge the truth behind the circumstances. What or who is at fault? What responsibilities do you have in the situation? What truth must you speak in love to another? What boundaries do you need to put in place to protect yourself from being hurt? Seek godly guidance and follow godly ways to resolve your difficulty.

STARTER PRAYER

Dear Lord,

Your love gives me hope and refreshes my soul. Help me become more self-aware so I can experience more of your love. Reveal my insecurities and weaknesses so I can bring specific issues and needs to you for help. Reveal the lies and destructive messages circulating in my mind, enslaving me to false standards and public opinion. Help me replace those lies with your scriptural truths. Soften and prepare my heart to accept the truth regarding _____ (personal situation). Please bring godly people into my life to help me resolve this problem. As I move through this situation, help me cast aside my self-protections and trust you fully with my life. May your healing touch reach into the depths of my heart and heal all wounds caused by this situation. Teach me to live victoriously.

May you be glorified by all I do.
Amen

Chapter 6

FORGIVENESS: HEALING AND GRACE

In the old rugged cross, stained with blood so divine,
A wondrous beauty I see,
For 'twas on that old cross Jesus suffered and died,
To pardon and sanctify me.

—George Bennard[11]

ANNIE SUFFERED A tremendous betrayal. Her husband had an affair with another woman. She was broken, despondent, and filled with bitterness, anger, hurt, and pain. She had lost hope for a restored marriage and prepared for divorce. As we talked about the betrayal, and delved into her emotions, I discovered she was abandoned by her father as a young girl. This early abandonment in her life created a fear of being left alone and abandoned in her marriage. She began to protect herself from these fears and insecurities by placing huge unspoken expectations upon her husband. She "expected" her husband to affirm his love for her in ways that she determined. When he spent time with her, she felt loved and happy. But when he spent time alone, she felt unloved, and responded with anger and silence. Days of silence would pass before the problem blew over. Eventually, Annie's husband became overwhelmed by his own fears and insecurities, and chose to escape from the situation by acting out inappropriately in order to cope.

Annie wanted to resolve her situation God's way even though she knew it would be difficult. As we continued meeting, she slowly began to understand her identity as a child of God. She embraced the truths of Scripture, spent time in prayer, and received healing in her heart from God's love. His love affirmed her belief of his presence in her. She grew confident in her knowledge that God would never leave her or abandon her. This newly felt security provided her the means to trust God with her fears. And the more she acknowledged her own insecurities, the more she began to understand the insecurities and fears of her husband. This helped her connect with him more intimately.

This couple decided to work out their struggles by including God in the process. With his help, they were able to put their marriage back together. It was not easy for Annie to forgive her husband. Trust had to be rebuilt in their relationship. That took time. Her main task was to forgive her husband. Her husband's main task was to rebuild her trust. And both had to deal with the issues in their hearts.

Forgiveness

Forgiveness is one of the most sensitive areas we have to deal with in life. It truly grieves my soul to hear so many painful stories filled with hurt and betrayal. I cannot think of anything harder on a heart than the wound that causes bitterness and lack of forgiveness. But living with an unforgiving heart devastates the soul, quenches the Holy Spirit within, and derails us from the abundant life.

If we wholeheartedly want to walk free of the issues that are enslaving our hearts, we must seriously consider the people in our lives we need to forgive. When forgiveness is practiced, the overwhelming burden weighing down our hearts is released because God renews the souls of everyone who walks through the process. Often our struggles with forgiveness happen because we don't really understand the forgiveness process. In order to appreciate the impact of forgiveness in our lives, we need to see how Scripture defines it.

Scripture describes two types of forgiveness. The first type of forgiveness is best understood as grace. When Adam and Eve disobeyed God they were found "guilty" of sin, which carried the "penalty" of death. If we look at this event, using legal terms, we find humanity on trial as the defendant in a judicial court case with God as the judge. Adam and Eve represented humanity because they were the first couple created for the purpose of cultivating the human race. Subsequently they were found guilty of sin and sentenced to death. Their sentence—death—was handed down to all of humanity because all future generations born from them came from their tainted seed. This death penalty covered both a physical death (death of the body) and a spiritual death (separation from God).

Jesus offered himself as a pure representative for humanity in order to appease the death sentence. He allowed himself to be sacrificed. His sacrifice satisfied the penalty of death that had been given to humanity. His death on the cross affected all of mankind because his action put humanity into the position where mankind could receive forgiveness. This is one of the victories of the cross.

Since Jesus took the punishment, the penalty of death, he holds the pardon that sets believers free. This is why forgiveness and salvation are given to those who believe in Christ. This is part of the gospel message. But as believers, we have been given so much more. We need to understand that an exchange took place on the cross. When Christ died he took our old, worn, tattered, broken, and sin-filled self and replaced it with a new person. I often ask people to write down what they think of themselves. Take a moment and think about that question. How would you describe yourself? Do you see yourself as too thin, too heavy, too tall, too short, too feeble, weak minded, strong willed, smart, loving, a bad person, a good person, a failure, lost, unforgivable? On the cross, Jesus took these self-made identity markers (the way we see ourselves) and exchanged them for his marker. This is how you are seen by God: HOLY, RIGHTEOUS, BEAUTIFUL, WHITE AS SNOW, A SON, A DAUGHTER, A SAINT, BELOVED, and most of all FORGIVEN.

Wrap your mind around the fact that God has forgiven you and sees you as holy and righteous no matter what choices you have made in life, no matter what your socioeconomic station, and no matter how many successes or failures you have experienced. This free gift of forgiveness is what separates Christianity from all other religions. It is the reason why grace is so precious. When the apostle Paul wrote, "God made you alive with Christ. He forgave us all our sins" (Col. 2:13), he used the Greek word χαριζομαι, which signifies "freely given." This word comes from the Greek root word χαρισ, meaning "grace." One of our prominent church tenets stipulates we have been saved by grace. We know this to be true because Paul used χαριζομαι, to describe God's gift of forgiveness. Grace is something that is given without any expectation of receiving anything in return. Restoration, salvation, and reconciliation with God are all gifts that are given by grace. They cannot be purchased by the things that we do (our works). We can express this type of forgiveness with one another by extending grace instead of judgment. If someone cuts you off in traffic, extend grace instead of anger. If the government moves in a direction you don't agree with, extend grace instead of rebellion. If someone in your family chooses to have an abortion, extend grace and kindness instead of unforgiveness and anger. If we cultivate an attitude of grace in our hearts, we will produce compassion, mercy, and forgiveness in our actions. Grace is one type of forgiveness described in Scripture.

Scripture also describes a second type of forgiveness. This forgiveness runs a little deeper and covers personal sin issues. Though we have been saved and forgiven in Christ, we are still responsible for perfecting our Christian lives. Giving and receiving forgiveness for personal sin issues is one of the ways we are perfected. Though we also receive this form of forgiveness from God, this is the type of forgiveness we not only can, but *should,* be giving one another.

This form of forgiveness is written with a completely different Greek word, changing its meaning. Matthew writes, "If you forgive men when they sin against you, your heavenly Father will also forgive you" (Matt. 6:14). The Greek word interpreted as "forgive" in this verse is $\alpha\varphi\iota\eta\mu\iota$. $A\varphi\iota\eta\mu\iota$ is more of a legal or accounting term. The Greek word suggests the concept of allowance, tolerance, releasing from the obligation to repay, canceling, or blotting out. The focus of the word is on the penalty—what is due—rather than on what was done (the sin itself). So our command to forgive is a command to release the sinning party from what they owe us.

OUR CALL TO FORGIVE

When someone sins against us, we are hurt emotionally and sometimes physically. Our hearts cry out in pain, and we want to see justice done. We want the person to suffer as we have suffered. So we either consciously or unconsciously attempt to make them pay. Sadly, out of the brokenness of our hearts, we often make ourselves or the innocent people in our lives pay the debt instead. Our demands for vindication may give rise to a life of isolation or a failure to build intimacy in relationship. Unforgiveness can drive men and women to withdraw, judge others, produce guilt in a spouse or child, remain silent, be controlling, and exhibit a host of other self-protective behaviors.

Unforgiveness and bitterness keeps us enslaved to our pain and brokenness by causing us to form a very unhealthy attachment to the person or event that caused us pain. This enslavement keeps us immature and unable to grow or move forward with life. It affects our ability to love others, understand the needs of others, and give of ourselves sacrificially.

The story of Jonah gives us a wonderful glimpse into bitterness (Jonah 1-4). This Old Testament prophet's bitterness and hatred for the people of Nineveh caused him to disobey God. His story is well known. He was the man who tried to run away from God, only to be swallowed up by a giant fish. Most people focus on his disobedience when telling his tale. However, I believe the real emphasis of the story is something found a little deeper within.

Looking closely at chapter 4, we find Jonah accepting a second chance to preach repentance to the people of Nineveh. But as we read through this chapter, we notice that Jonah was full of bitterness the whole time he was preaching repentance. He clearly held contempt for the Ninevites, even after witnessing the Holy Spirit's work in the hearts of the community. This attitude can be discerned because Jonah abruptly leaves the city instead of spending time there rejoicing with God over the entire nation's complete and utter repentance from evil and violent ways. Jonah walks away from the comfort of Nineveh, sits on a cliff in the hot desert, and hopes God will destroy them (4:5).

Jonah's dialog with God gives insight into his heart. His disturbing prayer reveals that his flight from God was not a random act of disobedience. He ran because he knew that God was full of compassion, slow to anger, and abounding in love (4:1-2). In other words, forgiveness is an attribute of God. Jonah didn't want to forgive the Ninevites for their sins against the nation of Israel. In his bitterness, Jonah cried out that he would rather die than live. Why would forgiving Nineveh generate such an emotional outburst? Possibly because Jonah had personally experienced their cruelty, witnessed their treacherous acts, or heard complaint after complaint about them from his own people. Whatever the reason, forgiving Nineveh made things personal for Jonah.

After confronting Jonah about his initial outburst of anger, God provided Jonah a plant that gave shade and comfort (4:6). Though happy for the gift of the plant, Jonah failed to thank God. Could it be Jonah felt entitled to have this plant? An attitude of entitlement often accompanies bitterness.

The climax of the story is revealed the following morning when the plant is destroyed. Again, Jonah expresses anger and a desire to die. God confronts this outburst a second time and asks him if he has a reason to be angry about the plant (4:9).

As we look closely, we find God confronting Jonah with the truth. The truth being that he had more concern for a plant than for 120,000 people who didn't know right from wrong. I believe Jonah showed concern for the plant because the plant provided him something. It gave him shade and comfort from the harsh desert conditions. This comfort left some feeling in Jonah's heart for the plant. However, he had no concern for the Ninevites because in his estimation, they were a despicable, unlovable people. They gave him nothing but grief. Therefore, he had nothing in his heart but bitterness to give back to them. A loss of compassion, concern for the welfare of others, and disregard for God's creation is a good picture of what bitterness looks like.

God is the Creator. We are the created. We should not be surprised that God has compassion for his creation. God clearly loves people, even those people who have sinned against us. Jonah's story teaches us three things. First, God will forgive our enemies if they repent from their sin. Second, God may choose us to deliver the message of repentance to our enemies. Third, an unforgiving heart will produce bitterness and sinful attitudes.

What Will Forgiveness Do for Me!

As we saw in Jonah's story, his anger caused him to make poor decisions. This contributed to his facing more difficulties in his life. Unforgiveness dries up the soul and makes us bitter. When our hearts are full of bitterness, we make poor choices that create more issues that must be handled. Keep in mind that a hard heart makes us dull to hearing God's voice, diminishes our ability to experience his love, and prevents us from growing spiritually strong. Forgiveness, on the other hand, softens the heart and helps us release control of our lives to God.

When we harbor unforgiveness, we undoubtedly try to control our situations and circumstances. Jonah tried to control his situation by running away, only to be swallowed up by a giant fish. How often have you tried to avoid the person who hurt you, only to run into him or her unexpectedly again and again? Perhaps the person who hurt you is a family member you can't easily avoid. What do you do then? Abandon your family? That can create loneliness real quick.

When we manage our lives to avoid people or keep secrets hidden, we give control of our lives (figuratively) to the person or event that caused us pain. The amount of control involved with managing our lives this way produces a tremendous amount of effort on our part. This effort keeps us living out of our brokenness. We blindly believe we have things well under control, but in actuality we are controlled by our fears and insecurities. Our fears place in our hearts an unhealthy attachment to a person or an event. Forgiveness allows us to heal from that unhealthy attachment by releasing the (figurative) hold the offending person or event has upon us.

Another point to consider is the fact that bitterness and unforgiveness inevitably lead to sinful behaviors. The consequences for sin are lost blessings in life. The apostle John describes God as being perfect love (1 John 4:7-8). Perfect love doesn't enable imperfect behavior. God directs us towards perfection by refusing to "enable" or bless destructive actions. If God blessed us when we sinned, it would give us a mixed message that says sin is OK under certain circumstances. Sin is never OK, but it can be forgiven. Here is another way to look at it. If God blessed us when we sinned, he would be rewarding bad behavior. God does not want us to become entrenched in destructive activities. That's why he will not reinforce those behaviors by rewarding them with blessings.

This point may be difficult to understand because we live in an enabling culture. We enable irresponsible behavior because we fail to deal with the truth. Sadly, our enabling ways nurture harmful attitudes and unhealthy behaviors that harden the heart. For example, I have heard parents comment that unruly children act out because "kids will be kids." When we enable our children to behave inappropriately by our failure to discipline, they grow up to become adults with hearts full of entitlement. This is a road that leads to destruction. God doesn't want us on that road. That's why he will not enable our sinful behaviors, and why bitterness causes lost blessings in our lives.

Forgiveness does a lot for us. It's a process that opens our hearts to the healing power of God, and it positions us to receive his blessings. Healing and blessings are gifts that greatly improve the quality of our lives.

How Can I Forgive When I Hurt So Much?

I understand the difficulties in forgiving someone who has hurt you deeply. I've had my share of pain. Even though Scripture sounds as if we are being told to stand there and take the abuse, rest assured that is not what it is saying. There are a couple of points to consider that help draw a better picture of what forgiveness looks like.

Keep in mind that forgiveness deals with the penalty of the sin, not the sin itself. If the sin against us were put into monetary terms, we would be asked to cancel the debt owed us. We are not to seek repayment.

Forgiveness Doesn't Mean:

1. **We Forget About the Hurt or Pain**. God is omnipotent, meaning all-powerful and all-knowing. He cannot simply forget a sin because that would contradict his omnipotence. Therefore, when God forgives personal sins, he chooses to blot out the penalty due as a result of the sin. In other words, once forgiven, he no longer holds the sin against us. When we forgive someone who has sinned against us, we are simply choosing to release him or her from any obligation to repay us for what he or she has done. We cannot change the past, or undo what has been done. When someone sins against us, we hurt. Our hurts are valid issues and must be healed by God. Forgiveness leaves us with two options. We can deal with the effects of the sin done in our lives or sin in return through retaliation. God asks us to follow his ways by trusting him and letting go of our need for retribution.

2. **We Are Letting the Hurtful Person Go Free**. Even though it may appear that the person who sinned against us is not being held accountable, that is not the case. We are releasing that person into the hands of God, who is judge over all. The apostle Paul tells us we are not to take revenge on those who do evil. We are to "leave room for God's wrath" (Deut. 32:35; Rom. 12:19). Solomon wrote, "Be sure of this: The wicked will not go unpunished" (Prov. 11:21). God is in control, and will deal with all sin his way and in his time.

   On top of everything else, the sinning party has to deal with the natural consequences of his or her actions. He or she may be arrested and sent to jail. This person may lose his or her marriage, children, grandchildren, job, or finances. Consequences follow all sinful behaviors.

FORGIVENESS MEANS:

- **Accepting the Wrongful Act Done Against You.** Forgiveness does not erase the effects of the sin or wrongful act. Healing from the sin must be addressed. The relationship must be rebuilt (if possible) and trust must be restored. When we forgive, we are making a choice to accept the sin done against us. We are accepting the pain, hurt, and the destructive behavior. We begin trusting God to heal our wounded souls. Boundaries and other safeguards have to be put in place when dealing with those who have hurt us and who have not repented of their sinful ways.

- **Healing Can Take Place in Our Hearts.** In order to heal, we must accept the pain and hurt in our lives. By releasing ourselves from an unhealthy attachment to the sinning person, we open our hearts to receive God's healing power and love. God helps us cope and endure the pain. He also gives us the grace we need to forgive the person who hurt us. These are part of God's blessings to us. He gives them to everyone willing to forgive. Forgiveness is not an easy process. God understands our struggles. This is why he supplies the grace needed to forgive. Apart from him, forgiveness is not something we can easily manufacture.

- **Spiritual Growth.** Adversity in our life develops spiritual growth if we allow God access to our wounds. The apostle Paul wrote, "And we know that in *all things* God works for the good of those who love him" (Rom. 8:28, emphasis mine). God is in control. He is sovereign. He is king over all of creation. He is the all-powerful being that keeps everything going. We grow spiritually strong when we acknowledge that God is in control of everything that happens in our lives. Believe it or not, God uses our wounds to perfect us. He cultivates something good out of every bad experience we undergo. Sometimes we get stuck in hard times because we fail to learn what God is teaching us through our difficult circumstances. When we fight the method God chooses to use in our lives, we remain stuck in our brokenness.

- **Asking Others for Forgiveness.** Our behaviors can be just as hurtful to others as their behaviors are to us. Growing in Christ also means taking responsibility for our actions as well. If we caused another's pain, then we must seek that person's forgiveness. If left alone, bitterness and unforgiveness will hinder our relationships and add misery to our lives.

Conclusion to Annie's Story

Annie had to work hard at letting go of the desire to receive payment (or retribution) from her husband for his sinful behavior. She had to stop reminding him of his sin. She was advised not to discuss his sin with others, not to bring it up every time they had a disagreement, and not to allow it to create a barrier between them. She was also taught to seek God for healing every time she felt her wound tugging at her soul. Her husband had to rebuild the broken trust in their relationship. He had to assure her that he had completely broken off his relationship with the other woman. He had to address her fears and pay attention to her feelings. He had to work hard at expressing his love for her. And he had to ask her and God for forgiveness.

After a few years of hard work, they now both agree their marriage is stronger today than it has ever been. This couple communicates better, prays together, and has grown spiritually strong due to their commitment to God.

This difficulty in Annie's life perfected her walk with Christ. She is now a strong and confident woman who has learned to express her fears openly with her husband. She has learned to speak the truth in love and receive the truth in love. She is grounded in her identity in Christ and feels his peace within her. Annie had to step out in faith and trust God with her husband, her marriage, and her ability to forgive. God's reward for her faithfulness included a stronger marriage, deeper faith, a new career (a bonus from her newly-found confidence), and a new focus in life.

Seeking forgiveness or asking forgiveness of someone is connected to confession. Confession is designed to bring relief and restoration with God, not guilt. It is an essential part of opening up our hearts to God and releasing the guilt, pain, and hurt we hold there. Confession is nothing more than agreeing with God that what we did, or how we have been living our lives, was contrary to his perfect design for us. Confession takes a weight off our shoulders and brings forth God's refreshing love. Do not fear confession. Embrace it and talk to God about the issues in your life.

Summing It All Up

Offering forgiveness is one of the hardest steps we have to take in our Christian lives. Our generation is so far removed from the fall that we experience sin behaviors more destructive to our emotional wellbeing than in generations past. Divorce, blended families, single parenting, alcoholism, abandonment, adolescent exploration of drugs, and sex are all commonplace today. In fact, so many men and women are inflicted with wounds at such early ages that by the time they reach maturity, their hearts are full of deep-seated scars. On the one hand, we want to leave our wounds at the foot of the cross. On the other hand, we want to see justice done. When we keep a tight grip on our anger, we become entrenched in unforgiveness. Unforgiveness gives rise to bitterness, and bitterness increases our pain.

Forgiveness is a crucial element necessary for keeping our hearts healthy. Forgiving the man or woman who sinned against us is not the same as letting the person off the hook, nor does it mean we are to be a doormat continually walked on. Forgiveness deals with healing the pain in our own hearts. Once we forgive, we release our built-up emotions on the offending person or event and open our hearts to God's healing touch.

Forgiveness often involves confrontation. Our job is to confront lovingly with the truth. We can't control how people respond to the truth, but we can make sure we are telling the truth. Boundaries and speaking the truth in love must be put into practice when dealing with an irresponsible person who continually offends. Praying for a forgiving heart is necessary when dealing with someone close who causes continual pain. A forgiving heart helps fight against bitterness.

The real question men and women want to know is, "How long do we have to put up with the offending person?" The disciples wanted to know the answer to this very question when they asked Jesus if forgiving a sinning brother seven times would be good enough. Jesus answered, "I tell you, not seven times, but seventy-seven times" (Matt. 18:21-22). In other words, Jesus is not looking for a set number of times we need to forgive others, but for us to *continually* forgive.

Unless we are in the midst of a life-threatening situation, we are to endure that situation the best way we can. Forgiveness allows us the means to prevent bitterness in our hearts. By trusting God with our circumstances, we can rest assured that he will deliver us when we have learned what he desires us to learn.

Steps to help you through the forgiveness process:

- **Pray Constantly and Continually**. Build up an intimate relationship with God. Invite him into your painful situation. Ask God for the grace to heal your heart and help you forgive the person who hurt you. Then watch and see how he provides what you need.

- **Speak Up.** Speak the truth in love. Let the offending person know how you feel when they cause you pain. If possible, offer a solution to the problem or situation.
- **Put Boundaries in Place.** If you have to deal with a repeat offender, put boundaries in place in order to protect yourself from excessive harm. For example, if a neighbor borrows things without returning them, let your neighbor know the next time he/she borrows your lawnmower you will be picking it up promptly on Thursday morning. Or if a friend habitually leaves her children for hours beyond what is discussed, let her know you won't watch the children again unless she returns at the appointed time. For further study in this area, I would recommend the book *Boundaries* by Cloud and Townsend.
- **Follow Through.** We lose credibility when we don't follow through with our established boundaries. The point behind confrontation is to lovingly bring the person into a position of repentance and personal responsibility. Structure is a very loving way to provide growth in people who were not raised with a good foundation early in life. Plan ways to stay behind the boundaries you put in place.
- **Seek God for Healing, Self-Image, and Love.** When we look to people or things for our identity, we entangle ourselves in a web of deceit. Allowing ourselves to be deceived by world opinion makes us vulnerable to offensive comments and poor self-image beliefs. Bitterness accumulates in our hearts simply by the way we see ourselves. We must seek healing for our insecurities and we must find our identity in Christ. When we are confident of God's love, we are able to forgive those around us who may assault us with worldly opinions and inappropriate comments.
- **If the Relationship Should End, End It.** If the relationship you are in leads you to destruction and sinful behavior, you

may need to forgive the person and end the relationship. For example, if you are involved in a relationship with someone who influences you to participate in unhealthy behaviors such as drinking, gambling, premarital sex, and viewing pornography, consider ending the relationship for your own wellbeing. Pray and seek guidance from God, who may want you to sever ties with this destructive person in your life.

REFLECTIVE THOUGHT

1. Spend some time in prayer asking God whom you need to forgive. Write down all of the names that come to mind even if at the moment you don't remember why certain names are there. Keep in mind that you may need to include yourself and God on the list. Be honest with God about your ability to forgive and ask him to help you release any pent-up anger or bitterness in your heart.

2. Read and contemplate the story of Joseph found in the book of Genesis chapters 37 and 39-50. Meditate specifically on Genesis 50:19-20. Then spend some time in prayer talking to God about your specific situation. Invite him into your pain and ask for healing from the wound caused by the sin you endured.

3. Spend some time in prayer asking God to identify the people in your life you have offended. Ask God the manner in which you need to seek forgiveness from these people. For example, do you need to write a letter, call, see them personally, or just confess the issue to God?

Starter Prayers

Dear Lord,

    Thank you for your love and forgiveness. Thank you for the grace you continually offer me. Search my heart and reveal the names of all the people who have hurt me. Help me begin the forgiveness process using the names on this list. I admit that I may not be ready to forgive everyone on my list, so please give me the grace I need to release any bitterness from my heart so I can forgive fully. Give me a forgiving heart so I can endure the sinful actions of people close to me. Teach me your ways through my pain so I can grow spiritually strong.

To you be the glory,
Amen

Dear Lord,

    Thank you for loving me and for forgiving my sins. I confess I have held onto resentment and bitterness toward _____ (person) for _____ (situation). I admit that I find it difficult to fully forgive this person, but I want to release him/her from the unhealthy attachment I have formed in my heart. In order to do this, I need your healing touch upon my pain. Strengthen me by your grace and enable me to release any bitterness formed in my heart as a result of this situation. Help me to learn from this situation, to set up good boundaries, and to remain faithful to you regardless of my situation. Give me a desire to have a forgiving heart and help me respond to hurtful people in my life with love.

To you be the glory always,
Amen

Dear Lord,

Please bring to mind the names of the individuals whom I have hurt so I can seek forgiveness. Forgive me for hurting _____ (name of person) by _____ (specific action). Guide me with your wisdom and help me understand the best way to seek forgiveness and reconciliation with this person. Strengthen me and encourage me to follow through with the method I must use. Remove the guilty feelings within my heart and heal my troubled soul with your grace.

To you be the glory,
Amen

Chapter 7

WISDOM FOR WARTIME

You said in your heart, "*I will* ascend to heaven; *I will* raise
my throne above the stars of God; *I will* sit enthroned on
the mount of assemble, on the utmost heights of the sacred
mountain. *I will* ascend above the tops of the clouds; *I will*
make myself like the Most High."
—Isaiah 14:13-14 (emphasis mine)

I T WAS THE middle of July, and I was doubled over in pain,
lying on my couch. The flu season was well behind me, yet
there I was sick to my stomach. I couldn't move without
feeling waves of pain. I had no warning for the onset of this flu.
One moment I was fine, the next I was down for the count. I was
extremely frustrated because everyone else in my home was fine. I,
however, had managed to catch the dreaded stomach flu. It didn't
seem fair. After lying on the couch in pain for a few days, I began
to pray for strength and healing. Wouldn't you know it, several
more days passed without any change to my health. So I decided to
stop asking for healing and started talking to God. I asked God if
there was something else I needed to understand about my illness.
I asked if I needed to let it run its course or if I needed to see a

doctor. I spent time with God seeking his guidance, not only his miraculous touch. To my surprise, I began to sense God asking me, "Why do you think you have the flu?" It had never occurred to me before that my illness could have come from an external force. After processing that thought a bit, I changed my prayers. My new prayers sounded like this: "Lord Jesus, in your name and in your authority, if any demonic force around me is causing my illness, remove it immediately and restore my health!" Guess what? I recovered the next day. My illness had come upon me within a week of my decision to co-lead a small prayer group. I will never forget my first leadership experience. It not only filled my heart with a passion for the hurting, but also taught me several tactics of the enemy.

All too often, I come across people who seriously underestimate the forces of evil. Some won't talk about Satan because they fear him too much and others won't because they don't believe he exists. I am here to tell you Satan and demonic forces are very real. We are not to fear them, but to learn about them so we can stand up against their schemes.

In the gospel of John, Jesus describes the enemy as a thief who comes to steal, kill, and destroy (John 10:10). This passage tells us a great deal about the nature of our enemy. When we unwittingly give ourselves away to temptation, the enemy steals our dignity and our hope. When we make mistakes, he kills our dreams. When we disagree with others, he destroys our relationships. He gives nothing and takes everything, leaving us poor, broken, and empty. Gratefully, Jesus doesn't leave us in despair. The second half of the passage informs us that he came to give believers a full life. Through Christ, we experience the restoration of our dignity and hope, are given the vision of new dreams, and are blessed with renewed relationships. Everything taken by the enemy is restored in Christ.

Why, then, do so many Christians fail to accept the things that have been restored by Christ? I believe the answer lies in our ignorance of the enemy and in our lack of faith. When our hearts are full of issues and attitudes, we give an opportunity to the enemy to steal back the freedom we have been given in Christ. The truth is that Satan and demonic forces have no real power over us other than what we give them. They cannot destroy us without our help.

Just Who Is Our Enemy?

Satan and demons are fallen angels. Angelic beings have been around since the dawn of creation. Satan was the most beautiful angel ever created by God. He was called the bright shining star, or star of the morning (i.e., indicating the brilliance of the sun, Isa. 14:12). He was adorned with jewels and stood in the throne room right next to God (Ezek. 28:13-17). In the same way that a crystal or prism reflects the spectrum of colors coming from the sun, Satan was to reflect God's glory to the universe. Unfortunately, he became filled with pride and aspired to be greater than God. Sin entered his heart. Sin originated in Satan. He stirred up a rebellion in heaven and was cast out along with one-third of the angels (Rev. 12:4).

The angels are free to choose obedience or rebellion. However, unlike mankind, the angels are not given a second chance (Matt. 25:41; 2 Peter 2:4). That is one of the reasons why fallen angels have so much contempt for humanity. They don't want to see anyone find the way to redemption. Misery loves company. Believers are a special concern to the enemy because we are the hands and feet of God. If we stumble, they can keep us from becoming spiritually strong and a powerful force for Christ. It is important to understand that demonic forces don't win battles by getting us to focus on them. They win battles by getting us to focus on ourselves. As long as we are the center of our thoughts (i.e., I am a failure. I am no good. I am better than the person across the street. I am entitled to be happy.), we spin away from God and remain enslaved to our self-centered nature.

TACTICS OF THE ENEMY

Even though civilizations evolve, temptations, desires, and needs remain the same. They just take on a current cultural twist. Rest assured that demonic forces cannot read our minds nor do they know our futures. They are, however, good observers. They faithfully watch one generation after another. They know our weaknesses. They know our struggles. They know our history. And they know our potential. It doesn't take much for demonic forces to figure out what buttons to push to make us stumble and prevent spiritual growth. Charles Swindoll writes, "Today's culture is corrupt. Humanity without Christ is totally depraved....we are now facing hardship, conflicts, and trials like none of us would have ever imagined because we are encountering our adversary on his turf. Everything God loves, he hates."[12] We see the truth in this statement played out all around us. Many marriages today end in divorce. Families are broken and our churches are divided because the enemy hates love and unity.

The enemy uses media and the entertainment world to assault us with inappropriate messages that con us into believing the world has something better to offer than what we can receive in Christ. Think about the onslaught of advertising aimed at youth and beauty. Men and women are targeted with deceitful messages that convey getting old as something undesirable. We spend an incredible amount of time and money in maintaining a youthful presence. This never-ending pursuit drags us away from God, leaving us vulnerable to one of the greatest lies of all—our belief that young, beautiful, and wealthy individuals are symbols of God's blessing. God has never been interested in those things. His focus will always be on the condition of our hearts! His blessings follow the purity of our motives and the righteous desires of our hearts. The longer we believe the lies of this world, the longer we remain toys at the mercy of demonic beings.

The forces of evil will use every possible opportunity to block us from succeeding in ministry and in life (2 Cor. 2:10, 4:4; 1 Thess. 2:18; 2 Tim. 2:25-26; James 1:14). The apostle Paul clearly points out that our struggles are not against flesh and blood, but against the rulers, the authorities, and the powers of this dark world, and against the spiritual forces of evil in the heavenly realms (Eph. 6:12). This passage divulges a huge battle zone filled with adversaries existing in a spiritual realm. My friends, we are at war against an enemy and dark forces we cannot see! We must be vigilant in our fight against these forces or we will unintentionally give the enemy opportunities to destroy all that we hold dear. Ground is always lost gradually. The first time a young man looks at pornographic pictures, or the first time a young woman gives herself away, vital ground has been seized by the enemy. Demonic beings use these activities and continuously taunt young men and women, thereby gaining more ground. In the blink of an eye, the purity in our hearts is replaced by desires for more forms of pleasure. Sadly, by the time we wake from our illusion of happiness our hearts are heavy and our minds are full of lies.

We do not have to live as victims of robbery. Every tactic used against us can be overcome in Christ. Jesus has given us authority to defeat the forces of darkness by our praying in his name (Luke 10:18-19; John 15:16). James commands us to resist the devil, guaranteeing that in time he will flee (James 4:7-8). The Greek word for "resist" implies that we are to hold our ground and withstand opposition.

The weapons of our warfare in this spiritual battle are resistance and drawing close to God. We draw close to God every time we pray, read Scripture, worship him, and obey his commands. The longer I stand up against adversity and temptation, the more I realize how weak I truly am. *I need to draw close to God if I am to fight this battle.*

When we recognize how powerless we truly are, we approach God with earnest needs. When needs are sincere and not aimed at frivolous desires, God graciously provides us strength and begins to fight for us in the spiritual realm. This is how we become victorious and overcome our weaknesses through his strength.

Even though we cannot fight the forces of evil on our own, we are not precluded from entering the battle. We have a responsibility to engage the war. We do this by speaking the word "no." *No,* I will not look at pornography. *No,* I will not gossip. *No,* I will not retaliate against the co-worker who provokes me. *No,* I will not allow bitterness to place a wedge between my husband and me. *No,* I will not...

Stepping into the Armor of God

In his letter to the Ephesians, the apostle Paul used the analogy of a soldier's armor to describe practical steps we can take to protect ourselves in the battle against the forces of darkness. Let's take a closer look at this passage and analyze each piece of armor:

Ephesians 6:10-18:
Finally, be strong in the Lord and in his mighty power. Put on the full armor of God so that you can take your stand against the devil's schemes. For our struggle is not against flesh and blood, but against the rulers, against the authorities, against the powers of this dark world and against the spiritual forces of evil in the heavenly realms. Therefore put on the full armor of God, so that when the day of evil comes, you may be able to stand your ground, and after you have done everything, to stand. Stand firm then, with the belt of truth buckled around your waist, with the breastplate of righteousness in place, and with your feet fitted with the readiness that comes from the gospel of peace. In addition to all this, take up the shield of faith, with which you can extinguish all the flaming arrows of the evil one. Take the helmet of salvation and the sword of the Spirit, which is the Word of God. And pray in the Spirit on all occasions with all kinds of prayers and requests. With this in mind, be alert and always keep on praying for all the saints.

- **Be Strong in the Lord** (v. 10): We are commanded to be strong in our faith. The Greek verb is written in such a way as to indicate that being strong in the Lord is our choice. This is an action that we need to do for ourselves, for our own wellbeing. This is an action that grows out of our response to God's love in our hearts.

- **Put on the Full Armor of the Lord** (v. 11): Again we find the command itself indicating an action we carry out. The Lord provides the armor, but we must put it on. In other words, God gives us everything we need to fight against the forces of evil, but if we don't use what he has provided, we stand unarmed. The command to put on the armor is for our protection because this armor is designed to help us withstand every attack that comes our way.

- **The Belt of Truth Buckled Around the Waist** (v. 14): The truth plays a pivotal role in our ability to stand against evil. Scripture tells us the Spirit of truth guides us into all truth, that God is full of grace and truth, we are to speak the truth in love, and that the truth will set us free (John 1:14, 8:32, 16:13; Eph. 4:15). We grow spiritually and emotionally strong when the truth is revealed because we gain insight and knowledge. Once this is discovered, lies no longer have the same power to enslave us because the truth overcomes them in our minds. The truth snaps us out of denial, grounds us in God's love, defeats the enemy, frees the enslaved heart, and makes us holy. Applying the power of the belt of truth to our lives means accepting the truths of Scripture and walking through life speaking the truth, hearing the truth, and living in light of the truth.

- **The Breastplate of Righteousness in Place** (v. 14): We have been made acceptable to God through the righteousness of Christ. We cannot work our way into righteousness. It is something that has been given to us by our faith. Since

Christians have already received the breastplate of righteousness, why are we so weak in expressing righteousness? It is simply because we don't really believe we are righteous. To stand strong with the breastplate of righteousness in place, we must accept the fact that we have been made righteous by Christ. Then we must choose to live in a manner that honors the righteousness he has furnished. Righteousness simply means to do right. We do right when we make good moral choices in life, when we treat people with respect and love, when we honor God through obedience, and when we observe ethical business practices in our jobs. There is nothing more freeing to the soul than walking through life with a clear conscience. The opposite is also true. There is nothing more powerfully enslaving to the heart than to carry the burden of a guilty conscience due to poor choices. The pursuit of righteous living keeps the breastplate of righteousness active in our lives.

- **Feet Fitted with the Readiness that Comes From the Gospel of Peace** (v. 15): Occasionally, I will go outside barefoot during the middle of summer. It doesn't take long before I feel like I am walking across burning coals. My steps quickly become erratic, and I frantically run inside for relief. When barefoot, I lose my ability to stand strong as I succumb to the pressure of the hot asphalt under my feet. I can honestly say I am very grateful for the piece of shoe leather (or rubber) that separates my feet from the ground. The simple act of wearing shoes radically changes my ability to withstand weather and terrain.

  When Paul talks about having our feet fitted with the readiness that comes from the gospel of peace, he is talking about immersing ourselves in the gospel message. When grounded in the message from the gospel of peace (the life, death, and resurrection of Christ equals reconciliation with God) we stand secure on an immovable foundation. Like shoes that protect our feet from the elements, this foundation protects us from being influenced by every form of deceit and false teaching we hear. When grounded, we are able to discern truth from deception, have a clear identity in Christ, and be equipped to handle the difficulties that come with discrimination, rejection, loss of a job, or financial problems. The simple act of grounding ourselves in the truths of Scripture radically changes our ability to withstand the pressures that accompany life.

- **Take up the Shield of Faith, With Which You Can Extinguish All the Flaming Arrows of the Evil One** (v.16): The shield of faith brings us back to belief and trust. Sadly, many of us have never really experienced the deep love and deliverance of God firsthand because we play it safe and never put our beliefs into action. We overprotect ourselves and our families by segregating into Christian communities. We must challenge ourselves to step beyond our personal comforts and trust God (not ourselves) with every aspect of our lives. Our belief in God must be partnered with trust if we are to experience peace, courage, and strength in the face of opposition. When we live with an imbalance between belief and trust, we carry an immature shield of faith and fall prey to the whims of demonic forces. These forces hurl a continual flow of flaming arrows upon us that can easily cause us to stumble, waver, and doubt our beliefs. These arrows come at us from the radio, TV, and through conversations with friends, family, and coworkers. These arrows are fashioned around our pain and weaknesses—personal areas of temptation, world philosophies, culture, lust, pride, religious beliefs, and a multitude of lies. We must develop a strong shield of faith so we can withstand the assault of arrows without being swayed by that to which we are exposed. Our shield of faith grows as we step out of our comfort zones and trust God more fully with our lives.

- **Take the Helmet of Salvation** (v. 17): A helmet is designed to protect the head. The protection of our head suggests that we must guard our thinking, especially our understanding of salvation. Salvation includes the forgiveness of sin, *all sin*—past, present, and future. Our salvation in Christ is the complete deliverance from the penalty of sin once and for all. No matter what you have done, no matter what you may do in the future, wrap your mind around this truth. *All* your sins have been forgiven. Paul wrote, "There is now no condemnation for those who are in Christ Jesus" (Rom. 8:1). The Greek meaning for condemnation indicates penalty. Paul is reiterating the fact that our salvation has removed us from the penalty or condemnation hanging over the heads of humanity. Just like righteousness, we have been given this helmet in Christ, but we need to accept (take) it. In other words, embrace the truth of our salvation. We are children of God who struggle with sin, but are no longer considered sinners.

- **The Sword of the Spirit, Which Is the Word of God** (v. 17): The Word of God is powerful! Passionately, Paul tells us the gospel message is the power of God for salvation (Rom. 1:16). In other words, deliverance comes though hearing God's Word. God's Word is alive and actively produces transformation in our lives (Heb. 4:12). It is sharper than a double-edged sword and cuts through the lies and illusions that fill our hearts. God used the power of his words to speak the universe into being and he will use the power of his words to bring it to a close (Gen. 1; Rev. 19:11-16). We have been given the greatest weapon of all time to fight the battle of evil in the physical as well as the spiritual realm. We have been given the Word of God. Memorizing Scripture rewrites the lies in our minds. Speaking Scripture causes the enemy to flee. Reading Scripture produces an immovable foundation within us. We are victorious over the enemy when we combat evil forces with the truths of Scripture. To sharpen this weapon in our life, we must spend time reading and absorbing scriptural truths.

- **Pray in the Spirit on All Occasions** (v. 18): In the spiritual realm our spirits are seated in heaven with Christ (Eph. 2:6; Col. 3:1), the Holy Spirit indwells us (2 Cor. 1:22; Eph. 1:13), and the Father pours his love into our hearts (Rom. 5:5; 2 Thess. 3:5). Whether we realize it or not, we are intimately connected to our triune God. Praying in the Spirit means to open our hearts to God and engage relationally with him. It means to pray earnestly and specifically from the depths of our deep-seated needs. It means to listen to the wisdom, truth, and guidance of the Holy Spirit. And it means to trust our Father to act upon and empower our prayers his way. Prayer is a gift from God. Every time we open this gift and speak to him, he responds by pouring out more of his love into our hearts. Keep your prayer life active and utilize this beautiful gift of communication God has graciously provided.

SUMMING IT ALL UP

The spiritual realm is a real, but intangible, realm that exists all around us. Satan and demonic spirits are free to move in and out of that realm at will. They take advantage of our disputes, arguments, unforgiveness, attitudes, and brokenness and use them against us. They manipulate us by using our issues to break apart relationships, cause division in our churches, disrupt our work environments, and stimulate rebelliousness within us.

As we become aware of our weaknesses and areas of vulner-ability, we gain an advantage over evil. Our awareness strengthens our ability to fight against unforeseen forces of darkness by calling on God for help. The apostle Peter instructs us to be "sober minded" and "alert" because our adversary prowls around like a roaring lion looking for someone to devour (1 Peter 5:8). If you've seen any nature program on the hunting practices of lions, you will understand the passionate warning within Peter's words. In a nutshell, the hunting tactics of lions are calculated and organized. They carefully observe and stalk their prey. Though a lioness can hunt alone, lionesses often hunt in groups in order to overpower larger animals. They move quietly in concert, encircling a herd of animals and then attack unseen. They are opportunistic, and timing is everything. When the assault begins, it's short and powerful.

Imagine now that you are the innocent prey. Satan, demonic beings, and forces of evil are prowling around looking for signs of ignorance, denial, and weak faith. These forces are opportunistic and encircle those with attitudes of entitlement, fear, anger, and rebellion. They move quietly in concert and attack under the cover of deception and half-truths. Before you know it, your anger toward your spouse has you in divorce court. Your fears force you to withdraw from neighbors and friends. Your attitude of entitlement justifies your pursuit of wealth and worldly success. The enemy has just devoured its prey.

Peter's instruction to remain sober (and alert) is a command given to protect us from evil by encouraging us to keep our minds sharp and focused at all times. To make his point, Peter alludes to the vulnerabilities associated with being drunk. When drunk, the mind loses its ability to exercise sound judgment, placing the individual at risk of making choices he or she may regret later. Because of this impaired position, a drunken individual is far more vulnerable to attack. In the same way, when our fears and insecurities fill our hearts and minds with destructive thoughts and attitudes, we become impaired. We lose our ability to exercise sound judgment and become easier targets to deceive. This deception causes us to dwell on our brokenness and run to our self-protections. Remember, the enemy wins when we focus on ourselves. Being sober minded means being aware of what's going on around us and within us. By understanding what triggers our fears and insecurities, we can stand up against attack and prevent ourselves from blindly dwelling on our weaknesses. Firmly believing biblical truths and knowing when to run to God for strength and healing prevents demonic forces from using our weaknesses against us and develops God-dependency in our lives.

The enemy doesn't want us to become dependent upon God, and he doesn't want us to grow spiritually strong. He tries to keep us hopelessly self-sufficient. But we have been given tools to fight him. Resistance and drawing near to God are two powerful weapons of warfare we have at our disposal. Those along with the full armor of God give us the strength we need to fight forces of evil in the spiritual realm.

In this world you will have trouble.
But take heart! I have overcome the world.
—Jesus (John 16:33)

REFLECTIVE THOUGHT

1. Look up the following verses: Job 1:6-7; Matt. 4:1; Luke 8:12, 10:18-19; John 8:44; Acts 10:38; Rom. 16:20; 2 Cor. 2:10-11, 4:4, 11:3, 14; Eph. 4:25-27; 1 Thess. 2:18; 2 Tim. 2:25-26; James 1:14, 4:7-8.

   a. What do you feel God is saying to you as you spend time reading his Word?

   b. Prayerfully ask God to reveal any area in your life where you may be experiencing deception from the enemy.

Take note of any patterns of behavior revealed that you believe may contribute to the enemy's attack in your life.

c. Finally, spend time in prayer, asking God to remove any demonic presence that may be surrounding you. Specifically ask for demonic forces to be bound and removed in Jesus name.

2. Find scriptural truths that counter the lies or areas of deceit Satan has been telling you. Write them out on a three-by-five card. Carry them with you and read them every time your mind hears the lie. For example, if you feel unloved, look up the following verses: Rom. 5:1-2, 8:38-39; Col. 1:21-22, 2:13; 1 John 4:9-10. If you experience fear: Ps. 56:3; Matt. 6:25-32; Phil. 4:6; 2 Tim. 1:7. If you fear abandonment: Ps. 37:28; Matt. 28:20.

3. List practical steps that will help you put on the full armor of God. Examples: Bible reading, special devotional time with God, memorizing scriptures, or a commitment made to God regarding ethical business practices.

STARTER PRAYERS

Dear Lord Jesus,

The circumstances of my life _____ (name specific circumstances) have left me feeling weak, broken, and depressed. Reveal the truth behind my emotions and bring healing into my heart. Help me see my self-protective behaviors so I can fight against them. Do not let the enemy of my soul use my brokenness as a weapon against me. Teach me what I must learn regarding this situation so I can stand up against his schemes. And if my mind is full of lies and deceptions, then direct me to the truth to counter those lies. Lord Jesus, I ask in your name that I be set free from demonic influences in my life by having them bound and sent into the abyss. Place your hedge of protection around me, my home, and my family. Heal the brokenness of my heart and fill me with your Holy Spirit.

In Jesus name,
Amen

Dear Lord Jesus,
    I confess that I have believed the following lies in my life _____ (name lie) and I ask your forgiveness. I realize my belief of these lies gave Satan the opportunity to steal precious ground in my life. I now want to reclaim that ground, Lord Jesus. Therefore, I ask for your help. Heal the brokenness of my heart so I can accept the restoration of my dignity, hope, vision, and future. If there is any evil presence around me that keeps me from accepting the truth, I ask that it be bound and removed from my presence. Lord, help me step into the full armor of God so I can stand strong against dark forces. Teach me your truths. May your truth set my heart free.

I ask these things in Jesus name,
Amen

Chapter 8

FROM FEAR TO FREEDOM

God gives us the vision, then he takes us down to the valley to
batter us into the shape of the vision, and it is in the valley that
so many of us faint and give way. Every vision will be made
real if we will have patience.

—Oswald Chambers[13]

WHEN MY BOYS were toddlers, they told me they were
afraid of my "angry voice." At the time, I had no idea
my voice sounded so scary. But the more I thought
about it, the more I wrestled with the notion that I was an angry
mom. I didn't want my boys to grow up afraid of me, so I asked
God for the truth. Was I really an angry person? I began to pray
for wisdom and understanding, and he very graciously showed me
the ugliness in my heart. It was true. I had an angry voice.

I was so wound up with fear and anxiety that when anything out
of the ordinary happened or when unforeseen obstacles ruined my
plans, I quickly became angry. The sad part was that I didn't see the
impact my behavior had on my children. When I took the time to
look, when I asked for the truth, I saw more than I wanted to see.
God not only showed me my temper, but also how my boys took

the brunt of my sin. I was pretty shaken up by what I discovered. Sin is devastating to our wellbeing. This is why it hurts others and why it makes us feel so bad. Sin is the reason we need such a loving Savior who desires to cleanse us from its damaging effects.

Once I stopped wrestling with the truth, I knew I had a choice to make. Should I avoid my problem or face it? Deep down I knew I couldn't avoid the truth. I knew I had to deal with my anger and with what lay underneath—my fears and anxieties. The first step to take in any situation, difficult or otherwise, is the step that leads to the truth. In my case, I had to accept my anger problem and ask God and my boys to forgive my unloving behavior. I began the healing process by taking responsibility for my anger. Then I prayed and prayed a lot.

Admitting that we are feeling hurt, have a problem, or are struggling with a sinful behavior is never easy. In fact it can be downright depressing. But just knowing what the issue that needs our attention is gives us an advantage. It's always an advantage to have something specific to work on with God because dealing with specific issues provides us the opportunity to experience his power at work, healing and cleansing us from our sin. Any time we *experience* God, we strengthen our faith (remember, faith equals belief and trust). When we don't bring specific issues to God, we remain hopelessly stuck in a superficial relationship. We don't get to know God intimately! We deceive ourselves into believing we are fine, when in truth we may be far from it. Therefore, any knowledge or clarity we acquire regarding our specific issues gives us power. In the very least, we learn what needs fixing and where we need to begin the fight.

Transforming the desires of the heart is essential if we are to heal and grow spiritually strong. The apostle Paul wrote, "Do not conform any longer to the pattern of this world, but be transformed by the renewing of your mind" (Rom. 12:2). A heart focused on self-protection is a heart conforming to the ways of this world.

But letting God transform the desires of the heart moves our focus off of us and onto him. Renewing our minds involves rethinking what we believe and how we live out what we believe. As chapter 5 discussed, the heart and the mind are connected. Even though the heart has precedence over the mind, the mind can still influence the heart by gaining understanding and knowledge. By accepting scriptural truths, thinking biblically, and obeying God's commands (which is living out what we believe), we open up a pathway into our hearts through our minds. Ultimately, we want to transform the desires of our hearts to want more of God and less of me.

Transforming the desires of the heart generally starts with self-discovery (discovering our issues). Battling what we've discovered involves every step that follows. Have you ever felt like your circumstances or issues were attached to a yoyo? We pray and give our problems to God one day only to discover them back in our arms again the next. Ever wonder why it's so difficult to stop a sinful behavior we don't want to have in our lives? The answer is tied to our hearts. In Paul's long and somewhat confusing narrative, he wrote:

> I do not understand what I do. For what I want to do I do not do, but what I hate I do. And if I do what I do not want to do, I agree that the law is good. As it is, it is no longer I myself who do it, but it is sin living in me. I know that nothing good lives in me, that is, in my sinful nature. For I have the desire to do what is good, but I cannot carry it out. For what I do is not the good I want to do; no, the evil I do not want to do—this I keep on doing. Now if I do what I do not want to do, it is no longer I who do it, but it is sin living in me that does it. So I find this law at work: When I want to do good, evil is right there with me. For in my inner being I delight in God's law; but I see another law at work in the members of my body, waging war against the law of my mind and making me a prisoner of the law of sin at work within my members. What a wretched man I am! Who will rescue me

from this body of death? Thanks be to God— through Jesus Christ our Lord! So then, I myself in my mind am a slave to God's law, but in the sinful nature a slave to the law of sin.

—Rom. 7:15-25

Paul uses this complex passage to explain the difficulties we face as we battle the desires of our hearts. He admits to feeling this powerful tug within his own heart, but he also tells us there is a way out—a way to fight the alluring draw of our sinful desires.

Paul tells us that the cross is the way out of our fears, troubles, and temptations. Being in Christ and sealed by the Holy Spirit means that every victory made on the cross by Jesus is *our* victory too. We acquired the victory the moment we said yes to Jesus as our Lord and Savior. In the letter to the Romans, Paul spells out the victory won in chapters 5-6, and in chapter 8, he tells us we have been set free from all condemnation. Make no mistake, chapter 7 lies in between these passages for a reason. Chapter 7 describes the reality of life in the world, the battle raging on within us preventing us from claiming the victory won through Christ's work on the cross.

The illustrations found on the next two pages may shed some light into the common problem we face, and our solution to that problem.

Our Problem:

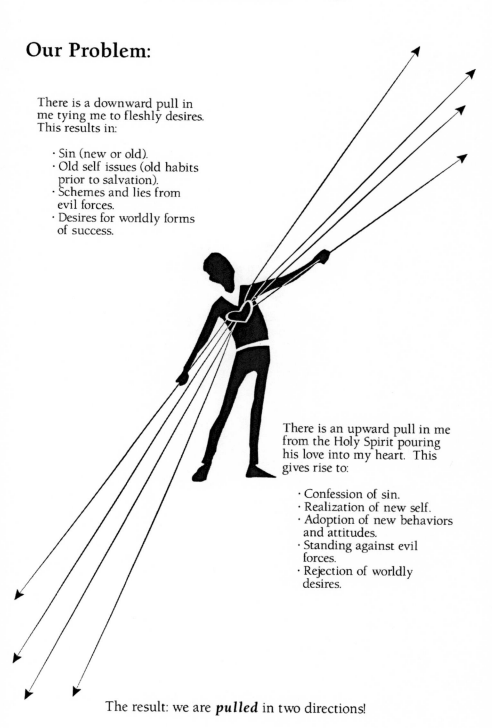

There is a downward pull in me tying me to fleshly desires. This results in:

· Sin (new or old).
· Old self issues (old habits prior to salvation).
· Schemes and lies from evil forces.
· Desires for worldly forms of success.

There is an upward pull in me from the Holy Spirit pouring his love into my heart. This gives rise to:

· Confession of sin.
· Realization of new self.
· Adoption of new behaviors and attitudes.
· Standing against evil forces.
· Rejection of worldly desires.

The result: we are *pulled* in two directions!

Our Solution:

Relief from the battle within our hearts comes through accepting the victory won on the cross.

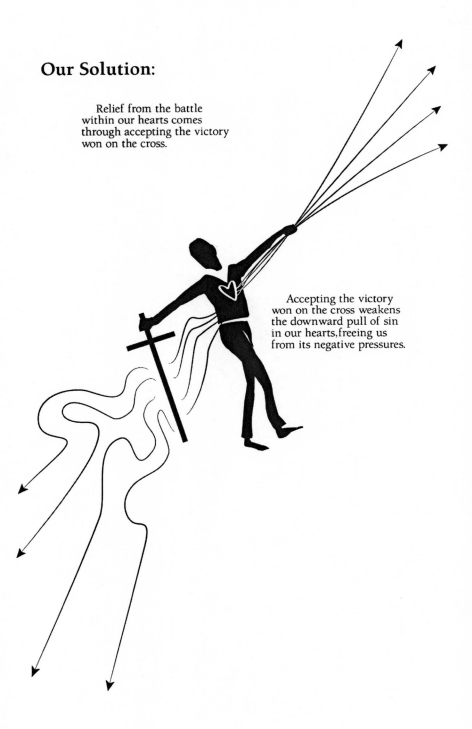

Accepting the victory won on the cross weakens the downward pull of sin in our hearts, freeing us from its negative pressures.

Chapter 7 is our warning bell, reminding us to fight and to take on the battle of our flesh because something far more enriching to our souls is within reach of our fingertips. The victory is ours, but in order to take a hold of it, we must trust God with our circumstances so he can help us overcome our flesh.

Here is how I trusted God with my anger issue. I made a conscious effort to learn about my frustrations. I ran to God whenever my emotions stirred my anger. I accepted responsibility for my anger every time I got mad. This meant apologizing when I sinned with anger, which happened a lot in the beginning. I spent a great deal of time in prayer with God. I talked with him, I pleaded with him, and I begged him to remove the anger from my heart. I specifically asked for healing that addressed my fears and anxieties, and for protection from the enemy so my anger wouldn't be used against those around me. I asked God to teach me what he wanted me to learn through my struggle. I also prayed for the Holy Spirit's intervention every time I felt emotional so I wouldn't go down the same behavioral pathway leading me toward anger. I clung to God and released control of my circumstances into his hands.

Then one day I noticed my anger was gone. I realized this after experiencing a very tense situation—a situation that would have normally triggered my anxieties and fears, but this time didn't. In fact, I remained calm throughout the entire ordeal. As I took a moment to process this achievement, I noticed something different about me. Deep in my heart, I had a sense of peace and calm such as I had never experienced before. My newly discovered inner peace was, and is, the power of God working in my life. I am still amazed whenever I walk through a difficult situation with tranquility. God is absolutely AMAZING! King David must have been talking about God's love and kindness when he wrote, "Taste and see that the Lord is good; blessed is the person who takes refuge in him" (Ps. 34:8). I truly feel blessed.

The greatest reward for my acceptance of the truth was that my children were no longer afraid of me. In fact, they don't even remember my having an angry voice.

CHANGING THE DESIRES OF YOUR HEART

By this point in the book you may have discovered a few things about yourself and may be wondering what to do with this knowledge. To help you fight against your protective desires, I have listed some practical steps you can take in order to bring what you've discovered to God for his transformational love. These steps help you apply the victory of the cross to your situation, enabling you to fight the desires of your flesh.

1. **Admit the Pain or Hurt** (John 8:32)

    Acknowledge the Truth. If you have been hurt by someone or have made a poor choice in life, let God into your situation by talking to him about it. Be up front with God. He already knows the details anyway. When we try to keep our problems or issues a secret, we prevent God from helping us through the pain. We also give the enemy something to use against us. Demonic forces not only use our secrets as weapons to convince us we are failures, but also to keep us living in fear of our secrets being made public. Living in the truth means trusting God with the truth of your situation regardless of who else finds out about it. You may need to discuss your issue with a mature Christian who can help you process your situation and pray with you.

2. **Keep a Teachable Heart** (Ps. 25:4-5, 51:10-12)

    a. *Be Willing to Look at Your Own Issues.* Keep an open mind and look for harmful attitudes, self-protective behaviors, unforgiveness, and bitterness hardening your heart. In other words, if your brokenness contributed to the situation, acknowledge it and prepare to deal with it as well.

b. *Accept the Truth.* Ask God to reveal the truth. Even though it may be difficult and contrary to what you want to hear, accept what God shows you and trust him to help you manage what he has revealed.

c. *Ask God to Teach You His Ways.* Study Scripture and learn what it has to say about your situation. Be willing to learn new behavioral pathways by exploring innovative solutions to handle your needs. This may include reading a book, attending a seminar, or joining a support group. Just be willing to learn.

3. **Seek Godly Solutions for Comfort and Wisdom** (Ps. 34; 2 Cor. 1:3-7)

a. *Pray for Healing from the Pain.* Ask God to heal your heart from the damaging effects of the specific issue. Remember, when we deal with specific issues, we experience God at work as he addresses our specific needs.

b. *Grieve the Loss* (i.e., relationship, parent, child, friendship, job, financial situation). Allow yourself to feel the pain by grieving openly with God over your particular issue. Allow God to comfort you *his* way as you explore your wounds with him.

c. *Read Scripture.* Scripture is a powerful tool God has given us to encourage, guide, reveal truth, and most importantly give hope. The Holy Spirit uses Scripture to teach, comfort, and settle our anxious hearts. Read it and believe it!

d. *Worship God Through the Bad Times.* Listen to praise music and thank God for his love even though you don't like your circumstances. No matter what is happening in your life, worshiping God will never leave you feeling empty.

e. *Find Someone Godly to Walk with You Through the Situation*. We have plenty of friends who tell us what we want to hear. These friends will agree with our anger or offer reasons why we should handle a particular situation our own way. But someone who will love you enough to tell you the truth and encourage you through the hardship is a rare treasure. These are the people whose support helps you grow spiritually strong.

4. **Walk with God Through the Difficulty** (Rom. 5:3-5; Eph. 6:10; James 1:2-5).

   a. *Do Not Go Around Your Problem*. No matter how difficult it is, face your hardship. Do not avoid or run away from adversity, walk through each issue dependent upon God.

   b *Cling to God and Move Forward*. Cast your fears and uncertainties onto God. Memorize the victories won on the cross (read Romans 5, 6, and 8), hold deceptive and negative thoughts captive, and fight against such lies with the truths of Scripture.

   c. *Don't Look Too Far Ahead*. Walk through your hardship slowly, taking it one day at a time. Don't expect to change every issue or behavior overnight. Rather, work toward a goal and make your effort manageable.

   d. *Relax and Know That You Will Have Good Days and Bad Days*. Don't give up hope. Some days may be harder on you than other days. Just cling to God and keep moving forward. Don't think that a bad day or a slip back into a protective behavior means failure. Just pick up the pieces and move forward again the next day.

5. **Let Go of Control** (Ps. 37:5-7, 46:10; Rom. 8:28)

   a. *Leave the Outcome of Your Situation up to God*. Don't expect or feel entitled to have the outcome of every hardship be in your favor. God may have plans for you that require you to endure an unloving spouse, lost job opportunity, or even an uncomfortable way of life.

b. *Don't Keep Trying to Get the Results You Want By Putting Extra Pressures on Yourself.* If you are exhausted from trying to fix your situation and still have no answers or peace of mind, consider changing your tactics or desired outcome. Ask God for guidance. Exhaustive effort often means you are not moving in a direction God would like you to move. Be willing to make some changes should God direct you to do so.

c. *Stop and Reevaluate Your Effort.* Periodically, stop and pray, seeking confirmation. Ask God if you are making the right choices, taking the necessary steps, and progressing in a manner acceptable to him.

6. **Remain Faithful to God No Matter How Long Your Hardship Lasts** (1 Peter 2:20-21, 5:10)

a. *Obey God's Commands No Matter What.* God's commands or statutes keep us focused on him and on holy living. They were designed to protect us and help us become the best human beings possible. His ways enlarge our hearts by filling us up with love for him and others. Though his ways may be hard and contrary to the bias of our flesh, they are the secret to peace and tranquility.

b. *Trust God to Deliver You When He Is Ready.* Walking through a difficulty with God is all about endurance and learning. When we have learned what God wants us to learn, he will change our circumstances.

7. **Pray, Pray, Pray** (Eph. 6:18; 1 Thess. 1:4-5; James 5:16).

a. *Pray Morning, Noon, and Night.* God has given us prayer as the means to communicate with him. This is a very precious gift that connects our hearts to his heart. When we pray, he responds with love. No matter what our circumstances, prayer never leaves us empty. Sadly, this beautiful gift often remains unopened. Why is it so difficult for us to talk to God? We should be on our knees crying out to him, pleading with him, and cherishing him with our words. But instead, we remain silent. When we seek the Lord with unwavering passion and desire, he will respond. Talk to God. Tell him of your pain, worries, fears, and struggles. Get to know him intimately.

b. *Lean into His Strength and Learn from Him.* Watch and see how God answers your prayers. King Solomon wrote, "Trust in the Lord with all your heart; do not depend on your own understanding" (Prov. 3:5 NLT). Rarely do we have all the facts or the big picture in mind when we face a struggle. Often our focus is on our own issue or need. Learn to silence your thoughts and listen to what God is saying. Ask yourself, "Am I willing to let God settle my issue his way, even if it goes against my desires?"

Summing It All Up

God uses our circumstances to reveal issues invading our hearts. If you ask him for the truth, be prepared to hear his answer in a variety of ways. Certainly he will reach out through sermons and Scripture, but, don't be surprised if your heart thumps when speaking to family, friends, or even while watching a movie. God wants our hearts, and if our issues get in the way, he gently nudges us to "clean house."

Discovering specific issues we need to work on with God gives us practical experience in interacting with him. It deepens our faith. Discovering areas of brokenness reveals places in our minds that need renewed thinking and protective behaviors in our hearts that need transforming.

When God exposes a painful issue, take courage and deal with it. We benefit so much from our pain. You see, the moment we began to protect our wounds and keep our secrets, we stopped growing, learning, and maturing. You see, when we were young and in the midst of difficult circumstances, we shifted our focus from problem solving to protecting and avoiding. We got stuck on the protective cycle and lost our ability to think critically or display sound ethics. These principles are normally nurtured during childhood, but many of us didn't get the chance to develop them, leaving us to learn them as adults.

When our current circumstances overwhelm us, it is usually because we don't have the skills necessary to resolve our situation. Learning problem-solving skills is necessary if we are to overcome our hardships. Since God works for the good of those who love him (Rom. 8:28), teaching us these life skills is one of the ways he uses our circumstances for our benefit.

Scripture instructs us to endure hard times because difficulties offer us so many benefits. I have listed a few of these benefits to encourage you to step out and face your problems rather than avoid them.

THE BENEFITS OF HARD TIMES

1. **Hardships Give Opportunities to Grow in Faith** (Ps. 18:2; 1 Peter 1:6-8). It is pretty hard to argue with firsthand experiences of God's faithfulness. The more we see God interacting in our lives, the greater our ability is to place our trust in him.

2. **Hardships Develop Our Strength and Endurance** (2 Cor. 6:4-6; James 1:2-4). Every time we conquer a problem in life, we gain knowledge and experience that carry us through to the next problem we face. Every hardship tackled helps us hang on that much longer the next time around. Just as

an athlete must build up muscle strength and endurance in order to win a race, we must build up emotional strength and endurance in order to win our battles.

3. **Hardships Develop Our Character** (Rom. 5:3-5). Our difficulties give us the opportunity to model problem solving skills to a world rapidly losing the art. Our integrity, honor, truthfulness, and faithfulness are tested every time we face hard times. What better way to witness Christ and the kingdom of God than by modeling his ways as we handle our pain?

4. **Hardships Cleanse Us from Sin** (Ps. 51; Heb. 12:1-2; 1 Peter 4:1). Hardships reveal our self-centeredness, unspoken expectations, feelings of entitlement, and so much more. They open our eyes to the ugliness we harbor in our hearts. This can be a very humbling experience. I know that I need to be humbled every now and then. Knowing what needs to be confessed starts us on a path toward healing.

5. **Hardships Perfect Us in Christ** (Phil. 1:6). The apostle Paul tells us that God started to work in us the moment we accepted Christ as our Lord and Savior. This work is designed to make us holy. When we avoid our problems, we not only interfere with this process, but also prolong our difficulties. Problems never really go away when we avoid them. They just keep coming back in new ways. We are victorious only when we face our issues. Each victory won brings us that much closer to Christ's likeness.

6. **Hardships Build God-Dependency** (Eph. 6:10; Phil. 4:13). Hard times build trust because they help us experience God's faithfulness. We need this experience in order to move from a mere belief in God to a heartfelt passion for God. A deep passion for God helps us exchange our self-sufficiency for God-dependency.

In life, we want to learn how to *respond* to our circumstances in a godly manner, not *react* to them out of our fears and anxieties. Gaining control of our emotions in the midst of difficulties helps us achieve that goal. When faced with difficult circumstances, our emotions should be used as a guide that alerts us to issues triggered deep in our hearts. Taking time to slow down and process our feelings while seeking God's wisdom and truth will help us learn and grow from our experiences. Discovering new ways to resolve our difficulties helps us respond to our circumstances better and better each time we face difficult predicaments. Growth and healing happen when we are determined to walk through our issues with God at our side.

REFLECTIVE THOUGHT

1. Read the following scriptures: Romans 5:3-5, 12:1-2; 2 Corinthians 1:3-7, 6:1-10; and James 1:2-4. What do these scriptures teach us about handling the difficulties in our lives?

2. Scripture is full of stories describing tragic lives. Many of the Old Testament narratives give detailed descriptions of broken relationships, immoral behaviors, addictions, murder, anger, rejection, fear, and feelings of hopelessness. These stories portray real people who suffered real-life issues. Their stories are encouraging because they illustrate God's faithfulness to broken and hurting people who seek his help.

   Read the narrative surrounding the life of Leah found in Genesis chapters 29-31, 35:16-19, and 49:29-31. Answer the following questions:

   a. How do you think Leah must have felt being told to marry (deceive) Jacob, knowing he had not chosen her to be his wife?

b. Leah struggled with being an unloved wife. Can you see growth in her faith over the course of time as she endured this hardship? Take a closer look at the names of her children found in Genesis 29:30-35.

c. What does Leah's story teach us about faith and obedience during hard times? And what does it teach us about God's faithfulness to the faithful? Hint: Which wife lived longer as Jacob's wife? Which wife had the firstborn son (something very important to the Israelite culture)? Through which wife did the Messiah's lineage come?

3. Meditate on Psalm 139:23-24. Spend some time in prayer asking God to reveal any behaviors in your life that may be hurting you and those around you.

STARTER PRAYER

Dear Lord,

How lovely are your ways! And how awesome are your commandments! They keep me grounded in your Word, protect me from harm, and comfort my soul.

Lord, please hold me tight and keep me close. I am afraid, but I want the truth. So search me, O God, and know my heart. Reveal any harmful issues within me and help me accept the ugliness you reveal. May your Holy Spirit guide me with wisdom and provide me the strength needed to accept the truth you show me and help me take the necessary steps to cleanse my heart from what is revealed. Please forgive me for hurting those around me with my destructive behaviors. Help me become a strong Christian with godly character by using my brokenness to perfect my soul.

May you be glorified by the transforming of my heart.
Amen

Chapter 9

FINDING PEACE *AMID* CHAOS

Faith is seeing that though I may live with scars
from healed wounds of the past,
God has incorporated them into his perfect plan for my life.
—Pamela Reeve[14]

TINA WAS SITTING next to her mother in the waiting room of the rehabilitation treatment center. The stress of dealing with her mother's alcohol problems had etched ugly marks all over her face. She looked so despondent that the check-in nurse assumed she was the one being admitted. Being told that her mother was the actual patient took the nurse by surprise because her mother was quite lively and acted as if nothing were wrong. After figuring out her mother's problem, the check-in nurse pulled Tina aside and said, "Your mother will be a very difficult person to treat."

Tina had grown weary from dealing with her mother's alcohol problem. For as long as she could remember, her father had avoided the responsibility, leaving her to pick up the pieces whenever things went bad. Since childhood, she had been the person who kept the family functioning.

Even though Tina was now an adult and had a family of her own, her biological family still counted on her to "fix" their problems. Lies filled her mind, telling her she was a failure because her mother had never changed. Tina was exhausted and she had no peace.

THE YOKE OF PEACE

Jesus says, "Take my *yoke* upon you and *learn* from me, for I am gentle and humble in heart, and you will find *rest* for your souls" (Matt. 11:29, emphasis mine). Jesus often spoke figuratively to help the human mind grasp kingdom concepts. Israel, being an agricultural community, would have quickly understood the picture depicted by the word *yoke*. We, on the other hand, must do a little research to grasp the intent or meaning of the illustration. A yoke was a harness that bound two oxen together, forcing the animals to work side by side. As long as they were bound together in the yoke, they remained under the farmer's control. So a yoke gives us a picture of two animals working side by side under the control of the owner of the yoke.

With that image in mind, taking up the yoke of Jesus implies being bound to his side and under his control. This means walking in harmony with him while surrendering to his lead. He assures us that his yoke won't be a burden because he is gentle and humble in heart and his yoke brings rest to our weary souls.

Experiencing the "yoke" of Christ involves learning his ways and applying those ways to our lives. This means allowing our hearts to be transformed and influenced by Christ and following the commands to love the Lord our God and love our neighbor. When living by our self-protective behaviors, we are not walking under the yoke of Christ. We are walking under the heavy yoke of our own self-sufficiencies. If we live under our own self-sufficiencies, we are rejecting Christ's influence in our lives, and thus are failing to love God and our neighbor in a manner suitable to him. Again we find we must look deeper into our hearts and discover the issues preventing us from binding ourselves to the yoke of Christ.

WHEN THE YOKES ON ME!

As it turns out, this verse from Matthew is more than just an invitation for rest. It digs deeper into the matters of the heart. Jesus used an Old Testament phrase in his invitation for rest. Anytime the Old Testament is referenced, a past situation is meant to shed light on a current point. To find out what Jesus intended to communicate through the Old Testament phrase, we need to take a brief walk through Israel's past.

When reading Old Testament narratives about Israel, we learn that the Israelites struggled with fleshly desires and worldly demands in the same ways we do today. They pursued wealth, survived natural disasters, divorced, had affairs, and suffered depression, illness, fear, and lost income and financial security. They handled their problems in a similar fashion as well. They denied, avoided, and looked for quick fixes. Basically, they were just like us. They wanted pain-free lives lived under their own control.

Tragically, not only did this attitude lead to unfaithful disobedience, but it also broke God's heart. This is what he said about the generation that lived at the time of the prophet Jeremiah: "From the least to the greatest, all are greedy for gain; prophets and priests alike, all practice deceit" (Jer. 6:13). God reached out to this generation and gave them a chance to be redeemed. He commanded them to return to the ancient paths, or godly ways, promising that in doing so, they would find *rest for their souls* (Jer. 6:16). Jeremiah 6:16 is the passage referenced by Jesus in Matthew 11:29. If we look a little deeper into what God was communicating to the Israelites during Jeremiah's day, we will discover a deeper meaning into what Jesus was communicating to the people of his day. The Greek word used for "rest" in the Jer. 6:16 passage suggests purification. It is important to note that this generation of Israelites had abandoned all godly ways and were worshiping foreign gods. They needed to purify themselves from their sinful ways. In the Jeremiah passage, God was telling the Israelites to purify themselves and return to godly worship. In doing so, they would experience his rest. In their case, rest included peace from battles by neighboring nations. Sadly, they wouldn't do it. They preferred to live their lives on their own terms. The outcome for these people was catastrophic. This generation was taken into captivity. They lost their land, freedom, and autonomy. Because they wanted ultimate control over their own lives, they chose to walk away from the gentle yoke of God, resulting in their coming under the heavy yoke of slavery, in this case from Nebuchadnezzar, king of Babylon.

Now as we turn back to Matthew 11:29 we see that it serves as a reminder and warning as well as an invitation. This passage tells us we sit at the crossroads of two choices. Bind ourselves to the gentle yoke of Christ, learn his ways (purify our souls), and receive his rest (relief and refreshment), or lose ourselves under the heavy yoke of slavery produced by the demands of our flesh (self-protective behaviors) and the pressures of this world (temptations and conformity). The yoke of slavery gives no rest!

THE UNRULY YOKE OF SLAVERY

A lack of faith and disobedience are reoccurring themes presented throughout both the Old and New Testaments. Understanding how these two topics affect us is essential if we are to bind ourselves to the yoke of Christ and receive his rest.

Another look into Scripture helps us grasp these kingdom concepts. This time we look to the book of Hebrews. The original readers of this letter were a group of Jewish believers struggling with real-life issues like fear, loss, and uncertainty. Because of their Christian beliefs, these people faced rejection from their Jewish

community on one side and persecution from the Roman government on the other. In fact, it's fair to say that these believers lived
under some pretty difficult circumstances. This letter was written
to encourage these readers to remain faithful to Christ and endure
their difficult situation. One of the arguments for perseverance
includes the promise of entering God's rest (Heb. 4:1-7).

There is no ambiguity from this writer. He starts his argument
with a clear warning: be careful or risk missing the opportunity to
enter God's rest (Heb. 4:1). To make his point, he draws us back
to Israel's past, reminding us of the fate of their ancestors. We are
taken to the generation of Israelites God delivered from slavery in
Egypt. These were the Israelites who followed Moses into the desert.
These were the Israelites who witnessed the miracles of God, saw
the plagues against Pharaoh, walked through the parted Red Sea,
and experienced God in the pillar of cloud by day and pillar of fire
by night. These were the people who were given the promise of
rest in the land of "milk and honey."

The Promised Land was the place of God's rest for the Israelites
freed from Egypt. This place contained a fertile strip of ground
strategically located in the middle of the desert. Rest for these
Israelites meant no more hunger, thirst, or aimless wandering in
the wilderness. It meant living in a place that offered bountiful
harvests, homes, and room to develop communities free from
attacking neighbors. But sadly none of the adult population (with
the exception of Joshua and Caleb) stepped one foot into the land
because they failed to develop any deep faith in God.

Regrettably, these people were also the ones who wandered
forty years in the desert until the entire adult population died. This
was the generation that experienced the mighty power of God,
yet fell short of receiving his rest because of their lack of faith and
disobedience.

We are told that the gospel message they heard was of no
value to them because they didn't combine it with any faith

(Ps. 95:6-11; Ex. 17:1-7; Heb. 4:2). The tragic details of their story tell us a great deal about their predicament. You see, these people witnessed God deliver them from one danger after another, yet the very moment they experienced thirst or hunger in the desert they complained and wanted to run back into the enslaving arms of Egypt. Their complaints reveal the true condition of their hearts. They had no gratitude in their hearts for God. They weren't thankful for what he had done for them. Their complaints made it clear that they didn't want desert living. They expected comfort and pain-free deliverance with little effort on their part.

Because their hearts were undisciplined and full of expectation, the promises given to these people were of no use to them. They weren't able to connect the miracles God did for them with the promises he gave them. They couldn't see beyond their own discomforts to grasp a future of promised rest. They couldn't imagine the future at all because they were completely absorbed with their own immediate needs. Despite everything they had witnessed, their faith in God remained shallow, preventing them from enduring the bad days.

In the same way, our faith is tested every time we face difficulties in life. If our faith remains shallow, we too will crumble the moment uncertainty or trauma comes upon us, preventing us from enduring our bad days. If we want to stand strong under the waves of adversity, then we must consider the issues in our hearts preventing us from developing a deep faith.

We have one more point to learn from these Israelites. God did lead these people to the threshold of the Promised Land. When the Israelites reached the wilderness of Paran, they were told to seize the land of Canaan, the Negev, and the hill country (Num. 13-14). God guaranteed their victory. But word spread throughout their camp that the inhabitants of the land were enormous and their cities fortified. It didn't take long before they felt overwhelmed and scared. Disobedience quickly followed. Instead of trusting God and boldly taking the territory, the Israelites chose to retreat in fear. In other words, they chose to self-protect rather than trust God. Because their faith was shallow, it could not withstand their fears. Their lack of any deep faith caused them to focus on their fears of the inhabitants over God's assurance of victory. God's response? "They shall not enter my rest" (Heb. 4:3, 5). God hates it when we don't trust him.

Hebrews 4 teaches us that when we focus on our misery, comforts, or lack thereof, our faith suffers. And when our faith suffers, it remains shallow, preventing us from enduring hard times and experiencing God's rest. This chapter also illustrates how easily the condition of our hearts undermines our faith and ultimately leads us to disobedience.

The author of Hebrews made his point by playing with the word "rest." He pointed to a literal place of rest (the Promised Land) and tied the loss of that rest to a lack of faith and disobedience, resulting in restless wandering in the desert. Though we may not wander around the desert today, we do experience restlessness as we seek happiness and contentment in life.

In the New Testament, God's rest is depicted as a spiritual rest or refreshment, culminating in a future place of eternal rest in heaven. The author of Hebrews is saying not to miss this point; we are not struggling through our difficulties in vain. Don't make the same mistake the Israelites made in the desert when they focused on their misery and lost their vision of rest in the Promised Land. We must endure our difficulties and live righteously because God has promised us refreshment today and a physical place of rest in the future. In other words, don't be so misguided by your problems that you lose sight of what lies ahead.

THE POWER OF GOD'S REST

God's rest for our generation does not include a piece of land for bountiful harvests and a reprieve from wandering. Today, Christ offers us something much deeper within—peace of mind, a guilt-free conscience, joy in our spirits, and the richness of his love. Today, his rest quiets the inner struggles afflicting our hearts and heals the wounds of our past.

God's rest enables us to endure difficult situations that would otherwise drive us crazy. It's like having an invisible shield surrounding our hearts, protecting us from the full impact of our worldly problems. In my own life, I find that his rest calms me in the midst of my struggle. It slows the anxiousness of my heart just enough, so I can think through my situation and respond with wisdom rather than react out of fear and brokenness.

Providing rest is one of the ways God sees us through our hardships. The story of the Israelites in the desert demonstrates his faithfulness to provide for our needs, especially when in the midst of difficult circumstances. For the Israelites in the desert, that meant food and water. For us, it means inner peace and refreshment.

Without this peace, we struggle through our difficulties apart from God. In essence, we labor under a yoke of our own making and end up running to our protective behaviors so we can cope. For us, lost rest is not the loss of a physical place, but the loss of inner peace. The battles we face today involve relational issues, financing, health, decision making, moral choices like abstinence, and issues concerning how we should spend our time. Our battles are ongoing issues that can emotionally wear down the strongest of souls. When we conduct our lives apart from God, our battles rob us of the refreshing power found in his rest.

The writer of Hebrews alerts us to our need of God's rest by concluding his point with these words, "Today, if you hear his voice, do not harden your hearts" (Heb. 4:7). With this passionate plea, we are reminded of the Israelites in the desert whose hearts were so hard they were unable to respond to God's love. The point is that we have the responsibility to respond to God's love with faith. When in the midst of difficult circumstances, listen for his voice and then heed his ways. Obedience and God-dependence are the ways we enter his rest. Jesus was saying the same thing when he said to take his yoke upon us and learn from him.

Tina's Story Continued...

Tina was not experiencing God's rest because she put a self-imposed burden (her yoke of slavery) upon her shoulders. This burden compelled her to keep trying to "fix" her mother's drinking problem. Tina used control as a form of self-protection, but the more she tried to control her circumstances, the more things happened that were out of her control, leaving her to walk through life broken and confused. Stress left her stomach tied in knots. Eventually, her constant involvement in her family's problems affected her health, her own family, and her faith.

In order for Tina to heal, she had to come out from under her yoke of slavery and bind herself to the yoke of Christ. This meant she had to learn about Jesus, his love, the cross, and the victory won on the cross. She had to renew her thinking by acknowledging her new identity as a beautiful daughter in Christ and by removing her old identity as "the fixer" of her family's problems. This took renewing her mind with scriptural truths, prayer, and self-reflection. Self-reflection is never easy, but is very necessary.

Tina also had to acknowledge the truth. She had to admit that she had no real control over her mother. She had to accept that her mother was sick and no matter what she did, Tina couldn't fix her. When she realized she was not responsible for her mother's choices, she was able to relinquish control of her family's problems. To be successful with this, she had to put strong boundaries in place, walk away from her protective behaviors, and learn to trust God with her life. She had to handle her problems in light of the truth and walk in a new direction with God at her side.

One evening she had a wonderful breakthrough after speaking with her mother on the phone. For the first time she stopped focusing on fixing the problem her mother called about and confronted her mother with the truth. This new way of speaking felt strange and uncomfortable, but it was freeing. When Tina hung up the phone, she felt a huge weight come off her shoulders. She felt excited and energized. God was strengthening Tina to walk through her problem and not around it.

As Tina began to grieve her losses (a healthy mother and childhood experience) with Christ and seek him for healing, she stepped onto the path that leads to God's rest. Her walk to freedom will not be an easy one, and she will face many challenges. Her family will fight her every step of the way because people hate change, especially when that change shines a bright light on their sinful behaviors. But as long as she stands her ground and depends on God to see her through, she will be victorious.

Summing It All Up

The testing of our faith always comes when we face great difficulties. The moment we feel uncomfortable, the true nature of our hearts is in view. It's amazing how quickly we forget the horrors of our bondages and prefer them as an escape from our suffering. Just think about how quickly we run to that brownie, drink, movie, or unethical action whenever we feel stressed. If our consciences are still working, guilt becomes a reminder of our slavery.

When we don't feel God's rest in our life, it's because we aren't ready to receive his rest, meaning we don't really want to be led by Christ. When our hearts are focused on our misery and a desirable way out of our misery, we aren't even open to hearing what God has to say. In fact, we tell ourselves things like, "This marriage is so bad that it can't possibly be God's will for my life, so he'll understand why I need to divorce" or "God wants me to be happy so why shouldn't I have a big house, a nice car, and all the fun things I can buy." The last thing we want to hear is endure, suffer, and stick it out, because God wants us to develop patience and character.

We must make a conscious effort to remember that our deliverance from slavery cost God the death of his own Son. We don't want to be ungrateful for this gift by focusing on our misery and demanding a rescue that satisfies personal desires. This was the mistake the Israelites made in the desert. They couldn't get past their discomforts long enough to realize the depth of love God had for them.

Can you accept your financial status, endure a loveless marriage, withstand a horrible job with an overbearing boss, and still love the Lord your God with all your heart, mind, body, and soul? Can you remain faithful, loving, and obedient to God no matter what terrible circumstances come into your life?

Disobedience robs us of rest. When we allow our fears to control our hearts, our fears tell us we can't trust God. Our fears will deceive our minds into believing that God doesn't have our best interest at heart. When we believe this lie, we turn to ourselves for our wellbeing and thereby increase our need for self-protection. Obedience, by its very nature, shifts our focus in life from ourselves to a love for God. Obedience gives us a course or direction to follow in life. This helps us fight the fear in our hearts. No matter what the situation, faith and obedience are the keys that open the door to our receiving God's rest.

The very moment we turn away from our self-protections and begin to live our lives dependent on God, he begins to purify our hearts from fear and sinful behaviors. As he pours his love into our hearts, we eventually fill up with his peace—his rest.

Jesus never promised us pain-free lives, but he did promise rest during the storm. Because of the world we live in, we will always feel some discomfort, pain, or confusion from our circumstances. However, God's rest takes the sting out of any pain or discomfort we face. Though our difficulties may afflict the body, they never penetrate the soul. The soul remains in God's rest—in his love.

Pray for a soft heart and the strength to endure the difficulties in your life. Walk through the steps outlined in chapter 8 and challenge yourself to fight self-protective behaviors that take you away from God's love. When you are willing to hear God's voice and follow his ways, you will enter his rest.

REFLECTIVE THOUGHT

1. Meditate on Matthew 11:28-30. Ask Jesus to reveal whether or not you are bound to his yoke and are on the path that leads to his rest. Journal your discoveries.

2. Is a difficult circumstance in your life preventing you from experiencing God's rest? Pray and ask God if you are experiencing a struggle with your faith (do you trust God with your circumstances) or a struggle with your obedience (are your fears keeping you from taking the necessary steps you need to take in your situation). Ask God for the strength to do what you must do.

3. Can you identify any self-protective tendencies in your life that if changed would deepen your faith and help you experience God's rest? If so, what are they and what steps can you take to change those behaviors?

STARTER PRAYER

Dear Lord,

Thank you for the yoke of peace you offer me. Surely obedience to your ways is the only way for me to live my life in a meaningful and healthy manner. At the moment, I don't feel your rest in my life. In fact I feel anxious, fearful, and full of emotions. I am overwhelmed by my circumstances and in need of your help. Please help me understand my fears. Reveal what is preventing me from experiencing your peace. Am I struggling to trust you with my circumstances, or am I afraid to take the steps of faith needed to move forward regardless of my situation? Heal the brokenness of my heart so I can stand up against my pain. Help me trust you with this difficulty in my life. Guide me with wisdom and clearly reveal what steps I need to take in order to walk through this situation. Please usher me into your rest and may I remain there eternally dependent upon your love.

Amen

Chapter 10

LIVING FOR TOMORROW

Aim at heaven and you get earth thrown in;
aim at earth and you get neither.

—C. S. Lewis

I DON'T WATCH a lot of sports, but I do love watching the Olympic Games. I will always remember the 2010 winter Olympics, not because of the number of medals won by the USA, but because of the personal story of speed skater J.R. Celski. This young man was competing in his first winter Olympics, and what makes his story so remarkable is the fact that he had a terrible accident just five months prior to the competition.

While competing at the Olympic trials held at Northern Michigan University, Celski crashed and found the blade of his right skate lodged in his left thigh. Though he made it through the trials, he was not expected to compete in the Olympics because of his injury. But this young athlete was determined to compete in the 2010 winter Olympics. He had his eyes fixed on that goal and would not let his suffering get in the way.

Celski's leg injury required sixty stitches and a lot of painful rehabilitation. This young man must have dealt with several bad days, to say the least. Just think about what he had to overcome: terrible physical pain, defeating thoughts, images of falling, fear of failure, and pressure to quit. His story tells me that no matter what he faced, he worked through his pain, because he achieved his goal of competing in the 2010 Winter Olympics. This young man surpassed everyone's expectations (possibly even his own) and won the bronze medal in the 1,500-meter event.

J.R. Celski is a great example of someone who endured his hardship, finished his race, and received his reward. Celski pushed through every difficulty he faced. He didn't give up, avoid, or deny the obvious. He had an injured leg, but he wouldn't let his injury stop him from working toward his goal. This young man kept his eyes fixed on the Olympic competition and the steps involved in getting there. He went beyond what most people would do and in doing so won an Olympic medal.

The apostle Paul often used athletic terms to challenge us to *run the race* of life in such a way that we run toward our heavenly prize. Paul told us to *endure* our difficulties so we wouldn't be disqualified and to *press on* toward a heavenly goal no matter what got in our way (1 Cor. 9:24, 27; Phil. 3:14). He was not the only writer who spoke about life as if it were a competition. The author of Hebrews wrote, "Let us *run with endurance* the race God has set before us *fixing our eyes* on Jesus the author and perfecter of our faith" (Heb. 12:1-2).

We have been given the hope, the dream, and the goal of an awesome future. Now the choice is ours. Are we going to enter the race?

KEEP YOUR EYES ON THE PRIZE!

An eternity spent with Jesus in heaven, free from all suffering and fear, is the prize set before us. If we keep our eyes fixed on Jesus and follow his lead, we will be successful no matter how painful our current crisis is. Saying no to premarital sex, loving critical and annoying people, tithing no matter how hard the financial strain, enduring cancer, or accepting the consequences for a sinful behavior are all ways to run the race with the goal in mind. Yes, it hurts to follow biblical ways, and we stand out when we do, maybe so much so that we become targets of abuse and harassment. All of our suffering is nothing compared to what is in store for us in the future. Our suffering will not be in vain.

How many of us view our Christian walk as if we were in a race? Really, what would it take to get you to push beyond what you think you can do? In Galatians 6:5, the apostle Paul speaks about bearing our own burdens, but not many of us come close to realizing the amount of burden we can bear because we give up so quickly and look for a way around the pain.

We are much stronger than we believe, and we have been given the Holy Spirit who empowers us. He is our teacher and guide. The Holy Spirit strengthens, comforts, and gives us the grace we need to handle any situation. We aren't expected to resolve our problems on our own, so why do we think we must endure on our own? God supplies the strength we need to endure any difficult circumstance! He carries us forward. He sees us through. Ultimately, he controls everything. We need only keep our eyes fixed on the goal set before us and walk in that direction.

FOCUS ON THE BIG PICTURE!

When it comes to understanding suffering and endurance, we must consider why and for whom we suffer. Are we suffering for our own personal gain and desires? Are we suffering for worldly possessions? Or are we suffering for Christ and righteousness? In this world we will suffer. So we must ask ourselves, "What does our suffering accomplish?"

When we struggle through life, focused on achieving success and happiness in this world, we become distracted. We lose our eternal focus and live solely for the comforts of this place as if our earthly life was all there is. Oh, how the things of this world tempt us to focus on them! Every message we hear from radio, TV, books, or people entices us to pursue happiness and the comforts of a "good life." However, a focus on worldly comforts puts us at risk of being deceived by spiritually blind advisors who easily convince us that their wisdom is superior to God's Word. Before we know it, our minds and hearts fill with worldly ways, and we begin to compromise our beliefs for the sake of our happiness. In the end, we let our suffering for the things of this world derail us from developing our faith. *We miss the big picture.*

Paul wrote that "all things are for our sake." The things he was talking about included suffering for righteousness (2 Cor. 4:15). That's why he encourages us to take heart and not let our problems, worries, or difficulties take our minds off our eternal future (2 Cor. 4:15-18). When our suffering motivates us to resolve our problems in a worldly manner, we need to stop and reevaluate the direction we are moving. We need to gain some perspective in order to help us understand the reason for our suffering.

To get this perspective, we turn again to Paul's writings. He describes our suffering as groaning and as a part of living in this broken world. Everything we see around us, including our bodies, is temporary. We must wrap our minds around the fact that there is nothing on this earth that can ever compare to our future glory. We subconsciously long for the eternal because eternity has been placed in our hearts by God (Eccl. 3:11). This internal longing is why we suffer and groan so much in the first place.

We can't help but suffer because we feel the temporary all around us. We see it in our bodies as they age, and we see it in the world as our natural resources are consumed. Outwardly, we see the temporary, but inwardly we desire the eternal. Failing to grasp the glorious nature of our future lives is the primary reason why so many of us fear death. This fear alone can keep our focus on the here and now. It makes us struggle to achieve all the fun, peace, and happiness we can get out of this world. But striving for what we can acquire here does nothing but leave us empty. If we aren't living in anticipation of our magnificent future with Christ in heaven, then we seriously misunderstand the reason behind all our groaning and suffering.

While trying to create a future focus in the Corinthian church, Paul used an illustration of our bodies to help distinguish between what we have now and what we will have in the future (2 Cor. 5:1-5). In this illustration, he describes our present bodies as an "earthy tent" of no value and our eternal bodies as "a building from God." He uses this illustration to tie all our groaning to a subconscious longing for our heavenly lives. Based on Paul's description, the following chart describes the source of all our groaning:

An Earthly Tent	A Building from God
We Groan: • Because we suffer in the tent—we are burdened with health issues, aging, pain, and brokenness. • Because we have been given new life but are temporarily living in old bodies. • Because we want our imperfect earthly lives to be swallowed up by our new eternal life in Christ.	*We Groan:* • With yearning for our perfect bodies. • With yearning because we long to be free from suffering and completely healthy, happy, and filled with joy.

Continued

An Earthly Tent	A Building from God
Distinction: • The earthly body is of no eternal use. • The earthly body will be torn down one day.	*Distinction:* • In Christ we have been given a promise for a new body, but we have not yet received it in a physical sense. • When our old body is torn down, or dies, we will be fully clothed in a new body because we will NOT be dead (1 Cor. 15:42-44). • We have been given the Holy Spirit as a pledge that this will take place!
Conclusion: We groan for what we have to tolerate here and now (Rom. 8:23).	*Conclusion:* We groan for what has been given but not yet fully realized (2 Cor. 5:17).

When we don't fully understand what's in store for us in the future, our suffering does nothing more than cause us to wrestle aimlessly with our earthly existence. Paul helps us gain some perspective by telling us to take heart. Suffering is part of living in a broken world. Suffering is the groaning of our hearts reacting to being housed in a decaying body that is living in a decaying world.

The fact is, we will suffer in one way or another as long as we live in this world. We don't want our suffering to keep us from running the race and achieving our goal. If we suffer for the fulfillment of our desires and happiness now, our suffering contributes nothing to our future lives because everything we acquire is temporary. If we suffer for Christ and righteousness, we build upon our eternal future in heaven. Now, I don't know exactly what that means, but Jesus told us that when we build up treasures in heaven they will not wear out, be stolen, or be destroyed (Matt. 19:21; Mark 10:21; Luke 12:33). His descriptions illustrate the eternal quality of these treasures.

Investing in our eternal futures is not a risky venture. On the contrary, Scripture tells us over and over again that enduring our pain, running the race, and living as if every day could be our last day on earth pays off with treasures in heaven. Since we are going to suffer anyway, shouldn't our suffering accomplish something greater than immediate comfort? Think about it.

FINDING HOPE

One of the reasons we look to worldly solutions for our problems is because we suffer feelings of hopelessness. Every time we take our eyes off the prize, our future eternity, we struggle in our earthly life. Our problems will consume us if we let our minds and hearts fill with nothing but fears, needs, and issues. We are told to fix our eyes on Christ and the eternal for our own protection. A Christ focus will always fill our hearts with hope.

My boys often ask me which holiday I like better, Christmas or Easter. My answer to them is always the same: "Christmas is wonderful, but it would be meaningless without Easter." Now don't get me wrong, I love Christmas. The idea that God would give up heaven and enter humanity for us is absolutely astonishing. God personally came to save us. That is true love! But where would we be if the resurrection never happened? What good would it serve us to endure our suffering if we had nowhere to go when our earthly life ended? The resurrection is the link to our final freedom from slavery. The resurrection fulfills God's promise for our perfect bodies. Christ led the way to our future by taking the first steps. His death and resurrection provided the tangible proof needed by the disciples so they could move forward with their faith. Our belief in that event, as recorded in Scripture, gives us something to cling to so we can move forward with our faith.

Our hope for the future comes from the victory on the cross. Jesus died for us and was resurrected to give us hope and an eternal focus. Our eternal life and future resurrection are promises first given to the Old Testament patriarchs Abraham, Isaac, Jacob, and David, and continue to be given through Jesus Christ, confirming God's intent to fulfill his oath. In fact, the writer of Hebrews tells us, "We have this hope as an *anchor* for the soul, firm and secure" (Heb. 6:19). The word "anchor" depicts something heavy that sailors drop into the ocean to keep their boats from drifting away. An anchor for the soul, then, implies being tethered to Christ, who prevents us from drifting into hopelessness.

Christ's resurrection shows us that something worth waiting for is coming for us in the future. The resurrection means that one day there will be an end to our suffering, imperfect bodies, poor health, and lonely hearts. The resurrection is the blessed hope Paul speaks about in Titus 2:13 and the living hope Peter speaks about in 1 Peter 1:3. The resurrection means that though the body may die, the soul lives on forever. The resurrection is why Jesus can say, "Do not fear those who can kill the body because they cannot touch your soul!" (Matt. 10:28).

When struggling, we should not place our hopes upon what this world can give us because the world does not give freely. It enslaves and draws the life out of us. We have been promised something far greater than we can ever imagine, and God has given us the Holy Spirit as the assurance of his promise. With all this assurance, can our lives ever truly be hopeless?

By focusing on Christ, his life, death, and resurrection, we have all the hope we need to survive the hard times. Therefore, isn't the thought of our glorious eternal future reason enough to live for Christ now rather than for our present existence?

SUMMING IT ALL UP

The existence of a physical place called heaven is definitely a hot topic. As believers, we claim to believe in heaven, but when it comes right down to it, we don't live like people who are convinced of its reality. We live more like people who aren't sure what our future holds. Our uncertainty forces us to spend our time trying to enhance our earthly lives rather than working toward our heavenly future.

In the book *90 Minutes in Heaven,* Don Piper describes his incredible journey to heaven and back. Piper is a man who knows without a shadow of doubt that heaven is a reality. He was in a terrible car accident—an accident that caused his death. The moment his body died here on earth, his soul woke up in heaven. These are his words: "Everything I saw glowed with intense brightness…It was as if each step I took intensified the glowing luminosity. I didn't know how it could get more dazzling, but it did…as strange as it seems, as brilliant as everything was, each time I stepped forward, the splendor engulfed me, and I had the sense that I was being ushered into the presence of God.…in heaven, each of our senses is immeasurably heightened to take it all in. And what a sensory celebration!"[15]

Not many of us will ever have an experience like Piper's, but then again not many of us would want to because once we enter the pearly gates of heaven who would ever want to return to this imperfect world again?

Our life on this earth is but a dot in time, even a hundred years is nothing more than a brief moment compared to all of eternity. Truly, our time on this earth is insignificant compared to the eternal life we are promised. Think about it! We are promised a future free from pain, suffering, and death—and a life that includes love, beauty, peace, and eternity (Isa. 11:6-9; Rev. 21:4). Every pure and beautiful thing God intended humanity to have will be fully restored one day. Wow! Won't that be incredible! Sadly, we seldom take the time to fully appreciate the magnitude of this future. Instead of looking ahead, we spend our time focused on how to get the most out of the world we currently live in. We settle for far less than God has in store for us. Don Piper's story shows us that something wonderful is within our reach, and reminds us that life here is *not* our final destination.

I realize that an eternal life in heaven seems far off and unbelievable when we are facing extreme moments of pain and unhappiness. I know it can be scary when we don't know how our bills are going to get paid. It is hurtful when our spouse has an affair. It is depressing when we are rejected by others. But the truth is, we have not been given this life to pursue personal happiness. We are here to love God and love our neighbor. That's why we must not let our problems take our eyes off the goal set before us. Like speed skater J.R. Celski, we need to accept our pain, endure our difficulties, and do everything within our power to move in a direction that honors Christ and righteousness.

Because eternity has been placed in our hearts, we will wrestle and groan over things like our health, marriage, body, job, and happiness. We can't help but groan because we long for perfection, but are temporarily stuck maneuvering through a decaying world. Asking the question, "For what am I suffering?" helps us determine the objective behind our suffering.

If our suffering takes us to worldly solutions and personal desires, we are suffering for our earthly lives. However, if our suffering leads us to righteousness, we are suffering for Christ and our eternal lives. For example, overworking in order to have worldly forms of success (big house, car, electronic toys, etc.), enabling the sinful habits of a loved one, or abandoning an unfulfilling marriage may produce rewards like wealth, peace, and happiness, but those rewards are aimed at improving our earthly life and can only be experienced now. They won't enhance our spiritual life or eternal future. On the other hand, if we live out biblical values and principles in our lives, such as refusing to partake in unethical business practices no matter the financial cost, confronting the sinful habit of a loved one, or enduring an unfulfilling marriage, we are suffering for Christ. Those practices enhance the richness of our spiritual lives now, and prepare us for our eternal futures.

Keep in mind that everything we see around us is temporary, even our suffering. That too will end one day.

Enduring our difficulties is never easy, but we don't have to struggle alone. God will carry us through from beginning to end. We need only ask for help and he will supply abundantly more than we can ever imagine, as long as we follow his lead.

Our ability to face the world with courage comes when we have hope. By keeping our eyes focused on Christ, his life, death, and resurrection, we find the hope we need to survive any difficulty. The resurrection of Christ was the example left behind to remind us that one day we too would have glorified bodies and new lives. This is a promise made by God and given to all who believe, and we have been sealed by the Holy Spirit as his assurance.

We have been given abounding hope in Christ so that we can stand strong in our faith. With such hope at our fingertips, shouldn't we set our eyes on the goal and exercise our faith regardless of the suffering we might endure?

REFLECTIVE THOUGHT

1. Spend some time thinking about your life. Do you think you are running the race with endurance for your heavenly future or are you living for the comforts of your earthly life? Journal your thoughts and discuss them with God for clarity and truth.

2. For what are you suffering? Does your suffering in life occur because you want to live for righteousness, or because you want success, peace, and happiness now?

3. Find some quiet time and contemplate Hebrews 12:1-2. What is God saying to you as you spend time reading this passage?

STARTER PRAYER

Dear Lord,

Thank you so much for the cross and for the richness of your love. Your life, death, and resurrection give me so much hope—hope that helps me endure the difficulties of this life. Jesus, I know you led the way for me to follow, and I so want to walk in your righteousness. Sometimes, however, I wrestle with the brokenness of my heart. I get scared from the hardships of this world and I confess that I let my fears control me. I want to be strong. I want to live for my eternal future, not my present life. Help me keep my eyes fixed on you, and help me persevere through my difficulties, equipped by your strength, wisdom, and love. I depend upon you to supply all I need to stand strong in my faith. Guide me toward biblical solutions for my problems and empower me to push though my hardships carried by your Holy Spirit. Help me work heartily toward treasures in heaven, rather than temporary riches on earth.

To you be the glory, forever and ever!
Amen

Chapter 11

PUTTING THE PIECES TOGETHER

Anyone who listens to my teaching and obeys me is wise, like a
person who builds a house on solid rock. Though the rain comes
in torrents and the floodwaters rise and the winds beat against that
house, it won't collapse, because it is built on rock. But anyone
who hears my teaching and ignores it is foolish, like a person
who builds a house on sand. When the rains and floods come
and the winds beat against that house, it will fall with a mighty
crash. (Matt. 7:24-27 NLT)

—Jesus

CARRIE WAS A very talented painter, but her brokenness
kept her painting scenes of darkness and tragedy. She could
never seem to get past the choices she had made when she
was young. Eventually, she lost all confidence and any desire to
paint. She became withdrawn. Carrie knew that God had already
forgiven her for her past, but she was not willing to forgive herself.
By holding onto unforgiveness, she prevented God's healing touch
from entering her heart. As she learned more about her brokenness,
she came to see how it had shaped her actions, thoughts, and ability

to experience any prolonged joy in her life. After a little more self-reflection, she came to realize God's amazing love.

Her experience walking through this process was like having a dark veil fall off her heart. She wept tears of healing and joy. She felt new life kindled within her heart. She picked up her paintbrushes and began painting once again. This time she painted lively scenes full of vibrant colors. She gained new confidence and found God giving her inspiration to paint wonderful images that communicated hope and healing. Carrie painted her way through her transformation. Her life took off again because she chose to accept her past, forgive herself, and allow God to heal her heart.

There is no doubt life is hard. Anytime we stand strong and face our difficulties, temptations, sinful behaviors, and personal desires with biblical values and principles, we suffer. Whenever I think about suffering, I imagine grueling pain and fearful interactions. With those thoughts in mind, it's no wonder people don't want anything to do with it.

Suffering will never be fun. In fact, I can pretty much guarantee that it will always be uncomfortable. That's why we don't like hearing the words "wait," "endure," "submit," and "consider the future." We'd rather hear words like, "Go ahead and find a quick remedy. You deserve to be happy."

Regrettably, our quick remedies often lead us to things like divorce, drugs, alcohol, food, or quitting a job. These so-called remedies, designed to keep us happy, usually add to our suffering in the long run. Once we start to "fix" our problems, we go on fixing and fixing and fixing every time we feel the pain. We never really get out from under our issues. We just drag them along with us throughout our lives.

The problem we face is, the longer we avoid dealing with the issues invading our hearts, the more entangled we become with deception and illusion. The truth gets lost somewhere inside us and we need intervention from the Holy Spirit in order to find it.

Even with his help, it may take years of steady work to untangle our messy hearts.

As long as we continue living under the control of our brokenness, we are enslaved! Our brokenness will control our hearts, minds, and actions. We deceive ourselves into believing we are free, but we are far from it. The only way to walk toward freedom is to recognize our brokenness and see it for what it is—fear, hurt, or some trauma in our lives. Freedom involves an exchange of our slavery to our brokenness for a dependency on Christ. By putting on the yoke of Christ, we learn godly principles to live by and have our brokenness used in a way that perfects us.

When we adapt biblical principles and values to our lives, and we depend on God to see us through, we cannot fail because our hearts line up with God's heart. He desires that we be successful when conducting life his way, that's why he guides us through anything we face. The more we step out with biblical values, the more we see God at work in us. This builds our trust and belief in him and moves our faith from shallow to deep.

ALLOWING CHANGE IN OUR LIVES

To walk free means to allow change in our lives. Change is not easy; it can produce a tremendous amount of suffering. Sometimes we suffer from the temptation to return to old protective behaviors because they have given us a false sense of security for so long. Other times we suffer because change makes us adopt new behaviors and forces us to learn different ways to maneuver through difficulties in life. Sometimes we suffer because we don't know how to apply biblical values and principles to our particular circumstances. All of these issues will be dealt with in time. God will empower us to overcome our fears, learn his ways, and set new behavioral pathways in our lives. We just need to take a deep breath, step up, and move forward in a direction pleasing to God.

Learning and growing involves change, and change inevitably involves suffering. Overall, the Scriptures instruct us to persevere *through* our difficulties. This suggests that God desires that we "suffer" a little.

Probably one of the hardest topics we must wrap our minds around is the fact that suffering is part of the purifying process of our hearts. Our suffering is a tool God uses to work out the issues that are hardening our hearts and preventing us from responding to his love. When we react correctly to our suffering, it should draw us into the loving arms of our Creator and not away from him.

We must keep in mind that God not only knows what we need in the physical realm, but also what we need in the spiritual realm, a realm that is a mystery to us. His solutions not only help us with our earthly existence, but are designed to enhance our spiritual lives. That's why our difficulties and fears are part of the purifying process. We need them to draw us closer to God so He can transform our hearts. The transformation of our hearts is an ongoing process that helps us grow spiritually strong, and it's a process that can be either easy or hard depending on how open we are to change.

Some of us come into a relationship with God in the same manner as the apostle John, the disciple who laid his head upon Christ's chest during the last supper (John 20:21). This man responded to Christ's love with love right away. He was the only male disciple we know of who didn't fear the authorities and who stayed with Christ throughout the crucifixion. His walk with Jesus was different from all the others, as his gospel testifies. Some of us, like John, seem to get it right away, and run into the loving arms of our beloved Savior. Those of us like John easily nurture intimacy with God.

However, others of us are more like the patriarch Jacob who wrestled with God. We wrestle our way into our relationship with God and we want to wrestle with him every step of the way. We wrestle with him over our desires, comforts, control, independence, need for success, and even how we worship. To those of us who choose to wrestle, God has to soften our hard hearts before we are ready to respond to his love and run into his loving arms.

The way we enter into our relationship with God is not important, but that we actively pursue a deep relationship with him is. We want deep interactions with God so we can grow inwardly full of his love and outwardly confident and self-assured.

So the question we must ask ourselves is this: Will we allow God to perfect us (transformation of the heart) using our circumstances as instruments of refinement or will we continue to fight him every step of the way by demanding happiness and short-term gain? Will we allow ourselves to be broken and miserable if that is what it takes to achieve healing and transformation?

I have to ask again, for what do you suffer? Are you seeking present happiness or a glorious eternal future? We must understand that what may be profitable to the soul, may take a toll on the physical body. Think about it. What will you do if your circumstances never change? Or what if God's will for your life is the terrible circumstance you are experiencing? Is his love alone enough to see you through this life?

We aren't promised happiness in this temporal realm, so we aren't entitled to always be happy. We have been given a promise that supersedes any present-day happiness. That is, we have been pledged as sons and daughters of God and heirs to his kingdom. Isn't our glorious future worth allowing change into our lives today?

CHOOSE TO WALK FREE

To walk free involves a willingness to feel your emotions and a readiness to hear the truth. This involves asking God to soften and heal the hardened places in our hearts. Keep in mind that when we feel, we experience more pain. We have become pretty accustomed to dodging our feelings, so this may be troubling at first. However, our emotions are the keys that open up our hearts so that we can experience God's love. We must be able to feel if we are to grow spiritually deep with God.

To walk free means to risk facing life apart from self-protective behaviors by trusting God instead. When we choose to walk free, we have the opportunity to maximize our lives and reach our fullest potential. This book was designed to be a tool that helps readers become more self-aware so that they can walk free of the obstacles that prevent them from developing a deep faith in God. To make the concepts easier to remember, the whole process can be summarized in three steps:

Step 1: **What Is Going on in Me?** When you feel emotional, face a difficult challenge, or start feeling fearful, stop and process. Spend time with God and ask him to reveal the truth behind your emotions. Find out why you are feeling the way you feel. Be observant and notice the details of the circumstances. Do the circumstances seem familiar to you? Have you had similar problems in the past? Perhaps you have to identify a pattern of behavior that needs changing. Perhaps you are grieving a broken area in your heart and you are in need of healing. Perhaps God is at work purifying a sinful behavior and it hurts. Be willing to hear the truth, pray for a soft heart, stay teachable, and be ready to listen to what God has to tell you.

Step 2: **How Am I Handling the Situation?** How are you reacting to the situation you are facing? Are you accepting the challenge in front of you? Are you confronting the sinful behavior by speaking the truth in love? Are you taking a risk by standing up for biblical principles and values? Or are you denying the truth, avoiding the issue, and escaping the pain? Pray and ask God to help you trust him with your situation. Ask for his courage, strength, and wisdom. Ask for the right timing before you confront a difficult person in your life. Make a point of stepping away from protective behaviors and toward biblical solutions. Deal with the issue rather than going around it. Grow dependent upon God and trust him to see you through.

Step 3: **Am I Keeping My Eyes on the Goal?** Am I willing to suffer for my eternal future? Are the ways I am handling my challenges, difficulties, and fears drawing me closer to Christ or moving me away from him? Am I letting my difficulties derail me from growing in my faith, or am I using them to keep me focused on heaven? Familiarize yourself with biblical principles and values and ask other believers how they adapt them to their lives. If these values were never modeled in the home you grew up in, they must be learned. Give yourself some time to learn them. It is easier to keep our eyes on the goal if we have established principles to live by. These principles become our life directives and the basis for our ethical judgments. Wrapping our minds around them helps us make quicker and more concise decisions. This helps us keep our eyes on the goal without having to think about doing it.

Concluding Thoughts

Our willingness to let God touch the wounded areas of our hearts starts us on the path to freedom. As we are guided through the healing process, we mature, develop, and literally grow up. Freedom is a byproduct of healing and spiritual growth.

One of the greatest benefits I have found from walking free is that once we recognize our brokenness, we are free to become the people we were intended to be. This is how we are able to maximize our lives. In other words, once our fears no longer hold us back, and our brokenness doesn't get in our way, God can mold us into the people he created us to be. The people we long to be.

I have spoken with so many people who are excited to discover or rediscover their talents. Some people I talked with mentioned painting the interiors of their homes with vibrant color for the first time. Others designed and planted a garden, discontinued excessive busywork, explored new job opportunities, volunteered at church, or went back to school. These may seem like simple things to do, but when fear and brokenness invade our hearts, we stop living. We get a mental block in our mind and we can't even imagine doing the simplest of things. We cling to our fears and not to God.

When we foster a mindset that embraces freedom, we will develop the strength to make mistakes without feeling like a failure. We will learn how to love and forgive those who hurt us. We will understand ourselves better and live more fully because a desire to walk free helps us make better choices in life.

People determined to walk free face their fears and meet each day clinging to God. They feel confident and open to receiving all that he has for them. They can hear God's voice and respond to his love even when feeling convicted of sin. The longer we walk toward freedom, the more our lives take shape and form.

The richness of God's love surrounds all who walk in his ways. The individuals who have applied the principles given throughout this book have developed a tremendous amount of trust in God. Because they have experienced his faithfulness in their lives, they feel confident to entrust him with their marriages, families, children, jobs, and futures.

As we continue to trust God with the circumstances of our lives, over time we will find peace, significance, love, self-worth, and contentment. This is the abundant life Christ came to give to all who believe. To walk free is a way of life, not a quick-fix solution. It takes time, patience, and endurance to master. However, intimacy with God and the transformation of your heart are well worth any effort involved.

At the beginning of this chapter I recorded from Scripture the parable of the wise man building on the rock because that story symbolizes the hard work necessary to walk free (Matt. 7:24-27). So I would like to close this book with one final illustration derived from that parable. I hope it helps you see how building on the rock may take time and hard work, but in the end delivers far greater rewards.

Building on the Rock	Building on the Sand
• Takes time. • Takes endurance. • Takes persistence and God-dependency. • Uses godly or spiritual tools. • Takes hard labor, a bit of blood, and won't look perfect on the outside. • Creates a stronghold.	• Takes the easiest/quickest way. • Avoids any real hardship. • Receives quick gratification. • Built with ease and self-sufficiency. • Uses the world's tools. • Looks great on the outside but empty on the inside. • Creates a flimsy shelter that falls when under any form of pressure.

Freedom starts with our willingness to risk walking away from our self-protections. When you are ready to take this walk towards freedom, God will give you the courage and strength needed to execute your new direction in life. Don't beat yourself up if you slip and fall back onto old protective behaviors. Just *don't quit!* Pick yourself up and start over again the next day. Each day is a new day with God, and his compassions are new every morning (Lam. 3:22-23). The key to success is to keep moving forward with God no matter what obstacles cross your path.

May your walk toward freedom be filled with God's love.

SUGGESTED READING
LIST FOR FURTHER
STUDY

Randy Alcorn, *Heaven*. Carol Stream, IL: Tyndale House Publishers, 2004.

Neil T. Anderson, *Victory over the Darkness*. Ventura, CA: Regal Books, 2000.

Dr. Henry Cloud and Dr. John Townsend, *Boundaries*. Grand Rapids, MI: Zondervan, 1992.

Dr. Henry Cloud and Dr. John Townsend, *Boundaries with Kids*. Grand Rapids, MI: Zondervan, 1998.

Dr. Larry Crabb, *Inside Out* . Colorado Springs, CO: NavPress, 1988.

Nancy Groom, *From Bondage to Bonding*. Colorado Springs, CO: NavPress, 1991.

Gregory L. Jantz, Ph.D., *Healing the Scars of Emotional Abuse*. Grand Rapids, MI: Revell, 2008.

Robert S. McGee, *The Search for Significance*. Nashville, TN: Thomas Nelson, Inc., 2003.

Ken Sande, *Peacemaking for Families*. Carol Stream, IL: Tyndale House Publishers, 2002

ENDNOTES

Chapter 1

1. Joel B. Green, Scot McKnight, I. Howard Marshall, ed., *Dictionary of Jesus and the Gospels* (Illinois: Intervarsity Press , 1992), 298-299.

Chapter 3

2. Dr. Larry Crabb, *Real Change Is Possible If You're Willing to Start from The...Inside Out* (Colorado Springs, CO: NavPress, 1988), 197.
3. Janet Geringer Wolititz, Ed.D., *Struggle for Intimacy* (Deerfield Beach, FL: Health Communications, Inc., 1990), 27.
4. Gregory L. Jantz, Ph.D., *Healing the Scars of Emotional Abuse* (Grand Rapids, MI: Fleming H. Revell, a Division of Baker House Co, 2008), 108.
5. Muriel L. Cook and Shelly Cook Volkhardt, *Kitchen Table Counseling* (Colorado Springs, CO: NavPress, 2006), 135.

Chapter 4

6. "Depressive Disorders." *Encyclopedia of Nursing and Allied Health.* Ed. Kristine Krapp. Gale Cengage, 2002. eNotes.com. 2006. 18 Sep 2010 <http://www.enotes.com/nursing-encyclopedia/depressive-disorders>.
7. Ibid.
8. Dr. Timothy Foster, *The Handbook of Christian Counseling* (Eugene, OR: Thomas Nelson Publishing, 2002), 86.

Chapter 5

9. Oswald Chambers, *My Utmost for His Highest.* (Uhrichsville, OH: Barbour Publishing, Inc., 1963), June 24.
10. Neil T. Anderson, *Victory Over the Darkness.* (Ventura, CA: Regal Books, 1977), 38-39.

Chapter 6

11. Rob Holt, Gen. Ed. *What the Cross Means to Me*, (Eugene, OR: Harvest House Publishers, 2002), 21.

Chapter 7

12. Charles R. Swindoll, *Why, God?* (Nashville, TN: W Publishing Group, 2001), 43.

Chapter 8

13. Oswald Chambers, *My Utmost for His Highest*, (Uhrichsville, OH: Barbour Publishing, Inc, 1963), July 6.

Chapter 9

14. Pamela Reeve, *Faith Is*, (Sisters, OR: Multnomah Publishers, Inc., 1994).

Chapter 10

15. Don Piper, *90 Minutes in Heaven*. (Grand Rapids, MI: Baker Publishing Group, 2004), 28.

WinePressPublishing
Great Books, Defined.

To order additional copies of this book call:
1-877-421-READ (7323)
or please visit our website at
www.WinePressbooks.com

If you enjoyed this quality custom-published book,
drop by our website for more books and information.

www.winepresspublishing.com
"Your partner in custom publishing."